LIVING JAPAN

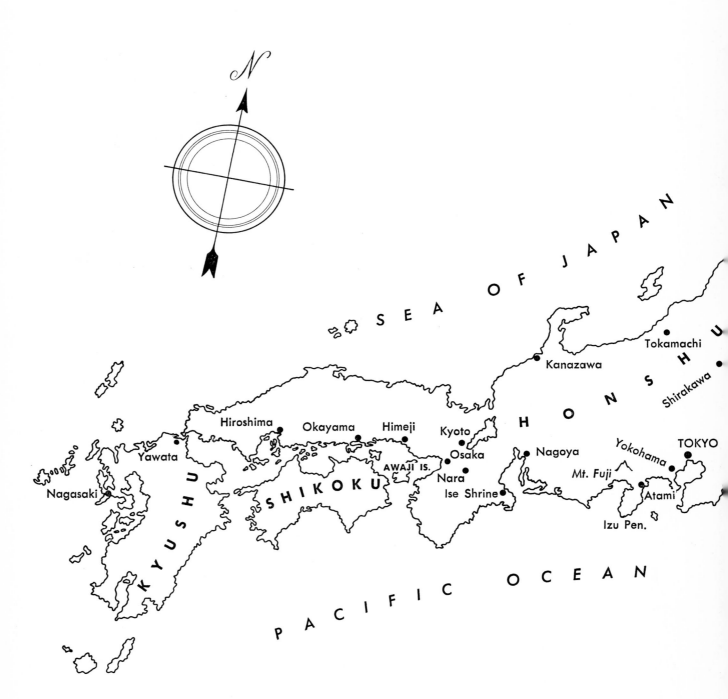

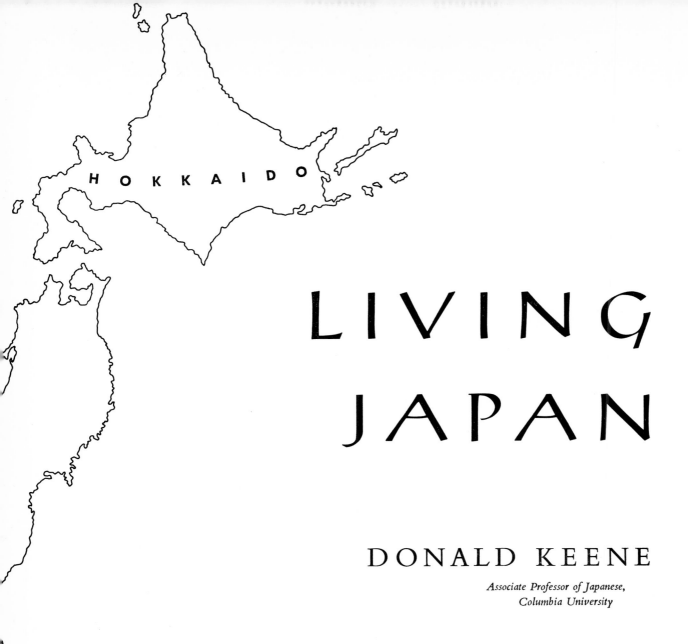

HOKKAIDO

LIVING
JAPAN

DONALD KEENE

Associate Professor of Japanese,
Columbia University

DOUBLEDAY & COMPANY, INC.

GARDEN CITY, NEW YORK

A Chanticleer Press Edition

Published by Doubleday & Company, Inc., Garden City, New York

Planned and produced by Chanticleer Press, Inc., New York

DESIGNED BY GEORGE SALTER

Printed by Conzett & Huber in Zurich, Switzerland

Library of Congress Catalog Card No. 59-10088

CONTENTS

INTRODUCTION

IN AN OLD CITY like Kyoto almost any day of the year brings a festival. As one walks along a back street with its rows of shabby houses and factories, one may suddenly hear shrill piping and the regular beat of a drum announcing the approach of a sacred shrine. The procession moves into sight: Shinto priests wearing gauzy cloaks thrown over their long robes; clusters of powdered and rouged children attired in much the same ceremonial raiment; musicians blowing flutes and horns; university students (hired by the day) grimly trudging along in medieval armor. The portable shrine itself, looking rather like a little house on a stretcher, goes lurching forward through the street, borne on the shoulders of a dozen men. Children of the neighborhood in black school uniforms trail behind the brightly-costumed procession. Another turn in the road, and they are all out of sight, though the music hovers in the air. In a thousand such ways the ancient past still invades the Japan of today.

The first view of a Japanese city is likely to be a disappointment to the traveler who knows of the country mainly the usual photographs of geishas posed on arching bridges, or who hopes to lose himself in the picturesque world which Lafcadio Hearn so magically described. He will find instead some of the less attractive forms of modern civilization everywhere: straggling suburbs reaching out to the airport; hodgepodges of concrete buildings inartistically surrounding the railway stations; grimy docks at the waterfront. Even when the traveler discovers something closer to the Japan of his dreams, it will not be exactly as he imagined it. In the remotest village there will be electricity and possibly television, and the doll-like *maiko* dancer may talk with greater feeling about baseball than about the flickering beauty of fireflies.

6

And yet, despite what at first must seem painful incongruities, the total impression is almost certain to be one of a land of great beauty, of a kind and charming people, of cities filled with an infectious vitality and villages where life still follows the immemorial cycle of the agricultural year. The traveler today may envy his predecessors of thirty or forty years ago who saw a Japan relatively unchanged from its traditional appearance, but the very contrasts of new and old have their fascination, and the knowledge that in another twenty or thirty years much of what is left today of the old Japan will have vanished lends poignancy to the scene.

The traveler can hardly be blamed if he prefers the old temple to the concrete office building or the sound of a solitary flute heard deep in the mountains to the braying of a loudspeaker at a public crossing. He is pleased when he finds a rustic farmhouse lighted with dim oil lamps rather than by fluorescent tubes. He may even think that he would prefer the Japanese to go on living in picturesque discomfort—at least for as long as he is there—rather than be surrounded by modern, hygienic improvements. But the traveler will find much to please him, even without condemning the Japanese people to perpetual servitude to the tourist industry. Some of the most beautiful cities, including Kyoto, Kanazawa and Nara, escaped destruction during the war and, despite self-inflicted disfigurements, still retain much of their old appearance.

The foreigner will probably prefer Kyoto, the old capital, to the modern metropolis of Tokyo. In this his taste will run counter to that of most Japanese, who think of Kyoto as a pleasant place for a visit or for a retreat in old age, but of Tokyo as the magnetic center of every aspect of modern Japanese life. Some Japanese, indeed, may with impatience cut short the lyrical praise bestowed by visitors on traditional Japan with a, "Yes, I suppose that is what a foreigner would admire." If they themselves were asked to prepare a book which would present the "real" Japan of today, they would probably fill it with photographs of shipyards and coal mines, printing presses and post offices. They might devote their major attention to describing the monotony and hardship of life on the farms, or to the poverty of mountain villages. They might report at length on the activities of labor unions and parent-teacher groups. They might, in fact, compile a large book of text and photographs without suggesting that Japan is one of the loveliest places on earth.

Such a book would be as misleading as its opposite number, the tourist guide with Mount Fuji framed in cherry blossoms on the cover. Although it is true that even for the inhabitants of an old city like Kyoto, the temple buildings and festivals affect their lives very little, the part which is touched even indirectly by the past is certainly the one which differs most interestingly from the lives of other peoples, and makes of a Japanese something more than a provincial European.

In this book, I have placed emphasis chiefly on what is traditional and uniquely Japanese in Japan today. At the same time, I hope that when the emphasis lies elsewhere, the modern setting will not be forgotten. A religious procession making its way past an automobile works is more exciting to describe than the factory, but the latter is unquestionably more important in the lives of most Japanese today.

In many ways this is a very personal book. It is based on my experiences during several years in Japan and colored by my affection for the country. Before committing any general observations to paper, however, I have usually looked for and found some Japanese authority who shared my views, for I know how easy it is for a foreigner to allow individual experiences to affect his conclusions excessively. If this were a different kind of book it could be copiously footnoted, though of course not all Japanese scholars would accept my findings. For example, one Japanese friend kind enough to read the manuscript pointed out that although I say that Japanese old people enjoy greater security than those in the West, the need for more homes for the aged is now being felt in Japan. This is unquestionably true, but another Japanese of my acquaintance, a sociologist who traveled through Europe in 1958, told me that he was so amazed to see how much worse old people are treated abroad that he had revised his opinions on the necessity of changing certain "feudal" Japanese customs. Both men's observations seem valid to me, but I believe that the latter is more characteristic, and have written in these terms myself. However, I recognize fully the existence of exceptions to my generalizations and am aware of the likelihood of change in a society as volatile as Japan's.

Like many another traveler arriving in Japan from the mainland of Asia, my momentary first impressions in Japan were that I had returned to Europe. The passers-by in the Tokyo streets were almost all in Western clothes, the shops filled with the paraphernalia of modern living, and the crowds pushing into the subways painfully reminiscent of those elsewhere. I recoiled from this aspect of Japan and might have remained buried in my studies of old literature and art had it not been for Japanese friends, particularly Dr. Michio Nagai, and Mr. Kishio Fuji, who first enabled me to understand how fortunate I was to be in Japan now of all times. That is what I would like to show in this book.

2

Chapter I

AN ISLAND COUNTRY AND ITS PEOPLE

2 "There towers the lofty peak of Fuji... it baffles the tongue, it cannot be named, It is a god mysterious."
(From the Manyôshu)

YAMATO, the ancient name for Japan, has been explained by philologists in many different ways, as mountain door, mountain tracks, mountain stop, and by other variations on the word *yama,* mountain. Probably no one will ever know the correct derivation of the name, but there can be no doubt of the rightness of the association of Japan and mountains. One is never out of sight of mountains in Japan, whether the low, gentle hills around Kyoto or the massive range of the "Japanese Alps" in the central part of the main island of Honshu. Most Japanese, indeed, have never seen the sun set except over mountains, or else over the sea. Viewed from the air, Japan appears a varied pattern of mountain landscapes, interrupted only here and there by patches of level land or lakes. Along much of the coast the mountains drop precipitously into the sea, or leave only a desolate fringe of shore. Scattered off the coasts, particularly in the Inland Sea, are numerous small islands, rising austerely like mountain peaks and suggesting the immense volcanic eruptions which originally, millions of years ago, lifted the Japanese archipelago from the sea.

"Countless are the mountains in Yamato," a seventh-century emperor wrote in a verse known to every educated Japanese—and supreme among the mountains is Fuji.

> *Lo! There towers the lofty peak of Fuji*
> *From between Kai and wave-washed Suruga.*
> *The clouds of heaven dare not cross it,*
> *Nor the birds of the air soar above it.*

The snows quench the burning fires,
The fires consume the falling snow.
It baffles the tongue, it cannot be named,
It is a god mysterious.

(From the Manyôshu, an anthology of the eighth century A.D.)

The ancient Japanese seem to have thought of mountains as the intermediary stage between earth and heaven, and the veneration they offered to Fuji in particular differed little from that accorded a deity. Fuji is not only the highest mountain in Japan but, by general consent, the loveliest. In almost every part of the country the most beautiful and impressive peak is called Fuji—"Sanuki Fuji," "Omi Fuji," "Ezo Fuji" and the like—whether or not it actually resembles the grandeur of the original Fuji.

Mountains have played an important part in the Japanese poetry of all times. The "marriage" of mountains has been celebrated, and numerous poems sing the praises of one or another mountain at each of the centers of Japanese civilization. In Japanese myths, the gods first descended from heaven to a mountain in southern Japan, and mountains have always been the most frequent sites for shrines. At the Kamo Shrine in Kyoto, for example, the altar stands before a mountain, and the mountain itself is the god enshrined. The belief in the sacredness of mountains persists to this day. A scholar of Japanese religion recently wrote, "Mountains are in fact (and not merely poetically) the spiritual homes of the Japanese. They are where the souls go after death, and, as the permanent gathering-place of the souls of the ancestors and the family gods, are the source of prosperity and happiness."

Some of the mountains are volcanic—Fuji itself was once so—and their eruptions must have inspired terror in the ancient Japanese. For the most part, however, the Japanese have not only worshipped but loved their mountains, and indeed the entire landscape of Japan. Japan is a country of endlessly beautiful panoramas. There are no deserts, no wastelands, but everywhere the green of a fertile and well-watered country. The very abundance of lovely scenery hides the real hardship of life in Japan; only seventeen per cent of the land can be cultivated, even with the infinite patience and labor of the Japanese farmer. Wherever the mountains open to leave a tiny valley, or even a pocket of land too small to build a house on, someone will have tilled it, and perhaps hacked terraces out of the mountains around it to gain another few feet of land. Life is hard for these farmers, and it has always been so; we with modern cynicism might wonder why the farmers venerated, instead of execrating, the mountains which left them so little land.

Thanks mainly to the mountains, Japan is one of the most crowded areas in the world. The Japanese themselves never weary of reminding the foreign visitor of the smallness of their country into which some ninety million people are packed, but by European standards Japan is quite a respectable size. It is somewhat larger than Germany, three times as large as England, and over ten times the area of Holland. It stretches from the latitude of Quebec to that of New Orleans. Because of the scarcity of level land, however, the parts of the country which may be easily farmed are extremely precious and utilized to the maximum. In terms of persons per arable acre, Japan has 5.5 to India's 1.7 and 0.3 for the United States. The extension of an airfield may mean disaster to dozens of families whose tiny farms are obliterated by the runways, and no amount of monetary compensation can enable them to find new fields. Since the war the land reform acts have broken up the great estates and made Japan a country of small landholders, but no matter how the land is divided, there can never be enough for the increasing population. Japan today presents a curious contrast of large areas of remote, scenically magnificent countryside, and small, congested sections of houses and farms.

For centuries the Japanese have faced the problem of living on an amount of arable land which has constantly dwindled as it came to be covered with the houses of a larger posterity. They have attempted to meet the problem by raising the yield of their land (it is now one of the highest in the world) and by the terrible practice of infanticide, widespread until recent times in the country districts. The population was kept down not only by deliberate intent but by the famines which ravaged the country periodically. For over two centuries, until Commodore Perry "opened" Japan in 1853, Japan was virtually cut off from the rest of the world, and a bad harvest inevitably meant that people died of starvation in large numbers for want of help from outside. Once Japan began to associate with the rest of the world, however, famines could be alleviated by imports of grain; infanticide came to be rejected for humanitarian considerations; and the improved conditions which followed on the industrial revolution led to a marked decline in the death rate as well as a rising birth rate. The growth of population has been spectacular since 1868, when the accession of the Emperor Meiji inaugurated a new era in Japanese history—in ninety years it tripled. The land could not accommodate all of this immense population, and farmers have continuously drifted to the cities in search of work, especially to Tokyo and Osaka.

Tokyo is by some estimates the largest city in the world, with a population of about ten million. Because of Japanese traditions and taste, there are relatively few multiple dwellings even in Tokyo; instead, millions of private houses, many of them extremely flimsy, are jammed against one another so chaotically that finding a given house, even when one is in the immediate neighborhood, is no simple task. It does not usually help much to ask directions of a passer-by, for the chances are that he will have just arrived in Tokyo himself. Certain parts of downtown Tokyo still retain something of the atmosphere of the past, but the city is full of newcomers. Second and third sons of farmers from the outlying provinces arrive daily in Tokyo. One of their favorite professions is that of taxi-driver; almost invariably ignorant of the location of even the most famous spots in Tokyo—the customer must direct them—they send their little cars racing through the streets with all but suicidal abandon. They are not simply reckless: they are desperately anxious to pick up even one additional fare; they may be exhausted and under extreme nervous tension at the end of what is often a twenty-four hour shift; and likely as not they live under the additional strain of conditions of extreme hardship and crowding. Yet it does not take long for them to consider Tokyo their home, and the village from which they migrated a few months before becomes only a place to visit at New Year or on the Feast of the Dead in August. The fascination of Tokyo for the country boy was celebrated by the great poet Bashô as long ago as 1684, when the city was still called Edo:

Aki tô tose	Autumn—this makes ten years:
Kaette Edo wo	Now I actually mean Edo
Sasu kokyô	When I say "home."

Some of the farm boys who come to Tokyo with such high hopes are forced by unemployment to return home, where, at least, they can eat, but this is a desperate last resort for most, and the city continues to grow. There is hardly a bus, a street, a department store in Tokyo which is not full of people from early in the morning until night. Every day of the year there seems to be a Christmas rush, and every night the main streets of Tokyo are as crowded as New Year's Eve in New York.

The visitor may wonder what they all do, how enough employment may be found in one city for so many intent, active people. The answer is given by any shop or office. The smallest branch of a bank, the most modest trading company, will have dozens of employees crowded into the narrow premises, desk against desk. Their jobs are not sinecures devised simply to take care of overpopulation. If nothing else, the intricacies of the Japanese language, which lends itself so unreadily to the typewriter, make it necessary to employ several people to do the work that would be performed by one stenographer in an American or European office. There are also girls whose sole function is apparently to keep a cup of tea filled in front of every customer and employee; girls to stand at the entrances to shops and bow a thousand times, ten thousand times a day, with the uniform greeting, "Thank you for coming to this shop"; girls to pass back and forth interminably on all the trains, sweeping, and selling sweets and soft drinks; girls to sit on either side of each customer at every bar (of which there are thousands in Tokyo); girls to wait behind the millions of pinball machines, listening to the billions of steel balls bouncing from pin to pin. There are, finally, factories where the employees laboriously and ingeniously make by hand items intended to be identical with machine-made products!

Some Japanese, particularly the more prosperous ones, deplore this pressure of people and live in distant suburbs or attempt to escape the city as often as possible for the quiet of the mountains. But one cannot be sure of finding solitude even in the mountains: in summer there are often long queues waiting to ascend the more popular peaks, and in winter one must fight one's way through forests of skis. The man who goes to a remote mountainside to hear the cries of birds or to see wild flowers blooming is more likely to find the debris from the box lunches of the hundreds of nature lovers who have preceded him. It is almost impossible to be sure of being alone anywhere in Japan. The only real privacy comes from shutting oneself off spiritually from other people who may in fact be a few feet away, and this kind of privacy is necessary in Japan. Fortunately, however, most Japanese seem to enjoy the very press of numbers, the sensation of being caught up in a crowd. Europeans or Americans walking along a busy thoroughfare will dodge elaborately so as not to bump into other people, but Japanese seem to make no such effort. The Japanese who visits the Meiji Shrine or the Emperor's Palace at New Year is probably there less out of piety or patriotism than in anticipation of forming part of what he hopes will be a record-breaking crowd.

The Japanese likes to think of himself as a lover of nature and of solitude. Some of the famous works of Japanese literature were written by men who chose to "abandon the world" and live as hermits, like the poet-priest Saigyô (1118–1190) who wrote:

Haruka naru	Living all alone
Iwa no hazama ni	In this space between the rocks
Hitori ite	Far from the city
Hitome omowade	Here, where no one can see me,
Mono omowabaya	I shall give myself to grief.

But for the Japanese of today nature and solitude are more likely to be found in a well-kept garden than on a mountainside. Few Japanese own or desire country residences where they can withdraw completely from their city friends. The Tokyo dweller is passionately devoted to Tokyo life, and when he goes away for the summer he is most likely to choose a resort like Karui-zawa where he can be sure of meeting a maximum number of acquaintances from Tokyo, and where the quiet streets of the town are lined with the local branches of familiar Tokyo shops. The country, the real country where farmers grow rice and wheat, evokes in the city-dweller (even in one of recent vintage) unpleasant associations of earthy odors, bad food, back-wardness, and all manner of inconvenience—not the delights of the simple, rustic life. Even the poets who celebrate the changing of the seasons and the beauties of nature usually live in Tokyo and make only occasional brief sojourns at the scenes of their poems.

For the young Japanese in particular the life of Tokyo is all but irresistible. The American from a small town or farm, rejoicing in the bucolic charms of the hinterland, is likely to opine, "New York is a fine place to visit, but I wouldn't want to live there." His Japanese counterpart will rarely have that kind of attachment for his native place. The village or the small town is lonely and dull, and the social relationships are bound by such complicated conventions as to destroy most of the joys of small-town neighborliness. Tokyo, indeed, offers the greatest chance of escape from the loneliness which is the dread of most Japanese. A Japanese psychologist has written, "The Japanese is by nature prone to feel lonely, and he cannot bear to lead a solitary existence. He does not wish to live except where he is constantly surrounded by people, whether his family or strangers."

The pleasure of crowds has its equivalent within the Japanese house itself. The boy from the country who finds a job in Tokyo would probably go out of his mind with loneliness if he lived like his London or New York counterpart in a room in a lodging-house where he may never see or hear the other lodgers and where he locks his door for privacy. The Japanese is more likely to share a room with several strangers, or, if he has a tiny room of his own, the walls will be so thin that he can hear every movement of his neighbors. He will soon become part of the "family." Each time he leaves the house he will be asked where he is going, post cards addressed to him will be read and publicly discussed, and an active concern in his personal life will be demonstrated by everybody. It is most unlikely that he will resent these intrusions into his privacy. There is, in fact, no Japanese word for "privacy," and the only words which convey the idea inevitably suggest loneliness or selfishness. Not only the word but the idea is unknown except to persons strongly affected by Western customs. The closest approach to privacy in a Japanese household is in the lavatory. The paper partitions which separate the rooms interfere with the passage of few sounds originating in the next room, but (as if to destroy even this shred of privacy) elaborately carved transoms in the homes of the well-to-do insure that the slightest rustle or cough will be heard. The doors of the rooms often have transparent panels, as if to facilitate observation of the interiors.

If the Japanese wanted more privacy, it would be perfectly simple for them to build their houses differently. Even the married couple who, one might think, would find it embarrassing for their every whispered word to be overheard, apparently find this embarrassment less disagreeable than the loneliness and isolation which a Japanese experiences in a locked room. Japanese who live in Western-style houses often leave the doors of the rooms open as if to preserve a mystic connection between the members of the family.

It is not only at home that the Japanese is indifferent to privacy. It is usually impossible to lock one's room (or even the lavatory) in a Japanese-style hotel, and the partitions are about as thin as in a private house. In the morning one performs one's ablutions at a hallway washstand next to strangers who may be stripped to the waist, and one is surrounded by their furious hawking and gargling. At night, particularly at a hot spring resort, one may be expected to share one's bath with strangers of both sexes. This is not the result of any shortage of water or plumbing; on the contrary, resort hotels proudly advertise baths which can accommodate a thousand people at the same time, and to bathe by oneself is considered a sad and lonely business. One of the great joys of the daily life of most Japanese is the neighborhood public bath where they meet their friends stark naked and enjoy the sensation of belonging to one big happy family. "Naked" festivals, at which men wearing only loincloths brave wintry blasts, huddling together for warmth, carry this love of contact with their fellow men to its highest pitch.

There are similar festivals even in the big cities where, however, the cherry blossoms arouse the greatest displays of enthusiasm. It really does not matter too much whether or not the blossoms are actually on the trees: the point of the festivities is to express one's appreciation for the idea of cherry blossoms by getting as drunk as possible with as many other people as possible.

The pleasure in such festivals is heightened by the fact that they—and the liquor which accompanies them—offer the best chance for breaking down the social barriers which cause loneliness. Although no privacy may be found within a household, a considerable degree of reserve towards strangers is required by custom, and normally, however lonely one may be, one must act as if outsiders did not exist. The cherry blossoms are the occasion for restoring one's fellowship with all men. Or, as the poet Issa (1763–1828) put it:

Hana no kage	Under the blossoms
Aka no tanin wa	Utter strangers
Nakarikeri	Simply don't exist.

A narration of the customs of the Japanese may make them appear a strange people, but this of course is likely to be true of any nation dispassionately examined from the outside. Travelers to Japan, even those most captivated by the country, frequently give vent to such hackneyed expressions as "You can never tell what they're thinking," and seldom try to discover the reasons for seemingly eccentric behavior. But even Japanese returning to their country after several years abroad are likely to feel out of place. The society and the country itself seem excessively confining, and the horizons narrow indeed. Japanese who study in a foreign country, particularly those who have spent their time there bitterly complaining about its ways and wishing they were back in Japan, may discover with a shock when they return home that they cannot live except in the near-Western atmosphere of Tokyo. They may actually find themselves looking at their compatriots in the manner of Takamura Kôtarô (1883–1956) when he returned to Japan from study in Germany:

Cheekbones protruding, lips thick, eyes triangular,
Face like a netsuke carved by the great Shuzan,
Expression vacant as though the soul were removed,
Ignorant of himself, jumpy,
Cheap of life,
Show-off,
Small-minded, self-satisfied,
Monkey-like, fox-like, squirrel-like, gudgeon-like,
Minnow-like, potsherd-like, gargoyle-faced
Japanese!

This harsh evaluation of his countrymen by a poet and sculptor is an extreme statement of something many Japanese feel on returning from abroad. There is a widespread feeling, particularly among intellectuals, that the Japanese are different from other peoples—"the orphans of Asia." Physically, of course, they much resemble their neighbors on the Asian continent, the Koreans and the Chinese. Despite assertions that it is possible to distinguish these races, mistakes are frequently made even by the Japanese themselves. What makes them feel so unlike Asians (or Europeans, for that matter) is not so much physical differences as their ways of thought or—to put the matter simply—their insularism.

Through much of her history, Japan has been isolated from the rest of the world, both because of geographical position and historical circumstances. Japan has sometimes been compared to England, another island nation, but the distance separating Japan and the Asiatic mainland is about six times as great as the Straits of Dover, and the journey from Japan to Korea was never lightly undertaken. Moreover, for very long periods Japan was closed to virtually all outsiders by deliberate policy of the government. During the two centuries before Perry's visit in 1853 the Tokugawa Shogunate, a military government which ruled Japan from 1603 to 1868, kept the country closed. Unlike England, Japan was never conquered by a foreign power and the only foreign influences on language, customs and institutions were those which the Japanese themselves chose.

The development in isolation had both good and bad features. To the good we may count the fact that the Japanese escaped being overwhelmed by the great civilization of China and were able to perfect their own unique arts.

3 *In 1872, only four years after the Meiji Restoration inaugurated an era of modernization, the first Japanese railway chugged the eighteen miles between Yokohama and Tokyo.*

3

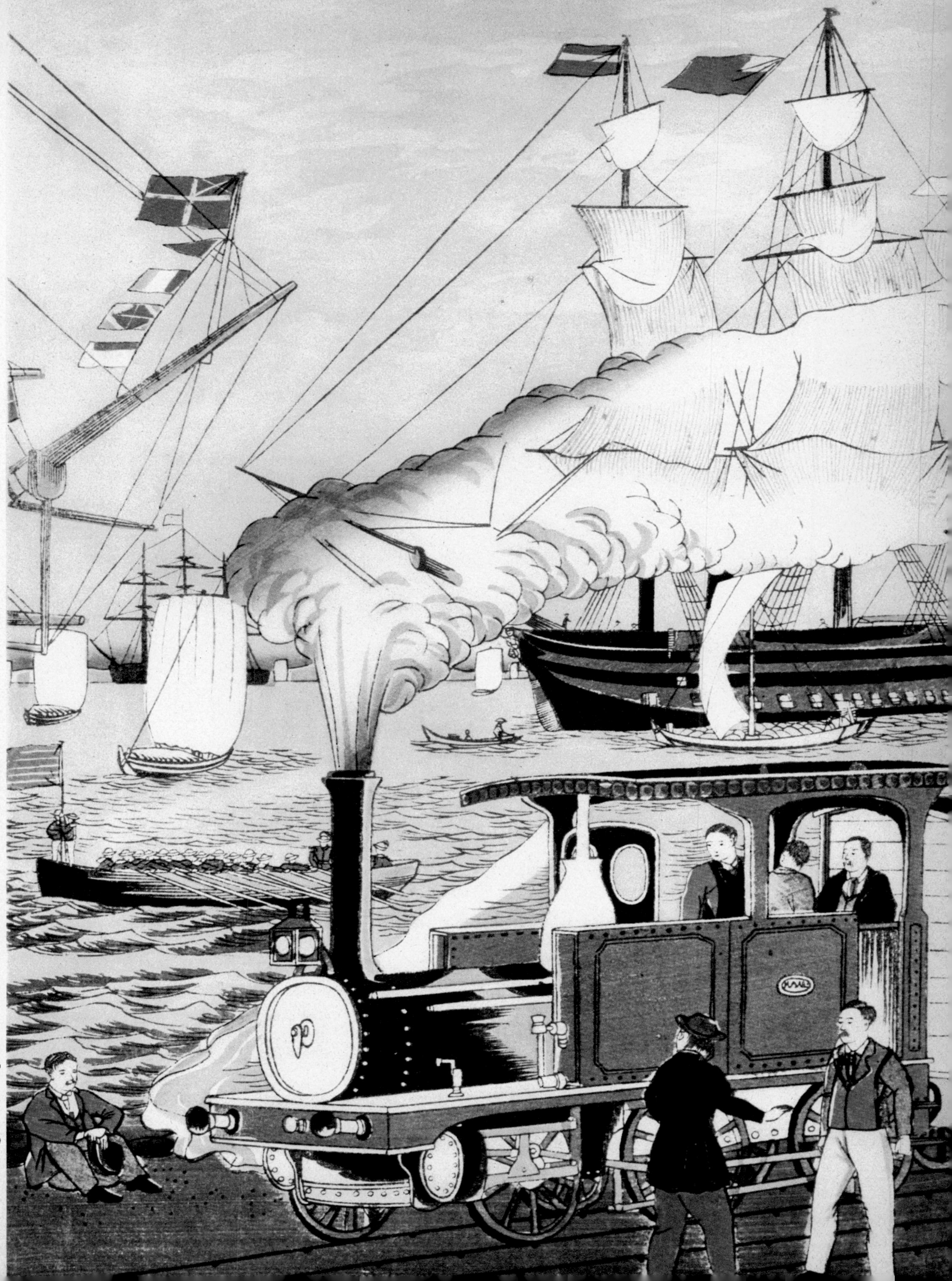

Library of Congress

彼理像
督マッチウ○セ
美辣水師提
盛頃斐謨
其和政治華
北亞墨利加

アーナホール
ボーフスブカナン
アーダムス像

4

5

KANAGAKI ROBUN

However, the long periods of turning inwards to their own resources inevitably produced a certain meagreness in artistic expression, and the insularism which the Japanese themselves so deplore. The immensely complicated Japanese language has reinforced this insularism, and even today the Japanese are accustomed to hide behind their language's protecting walls. So few foreigners master the language that the Japanese feel safe within it, able to tell secrets to ninety million people without the fear of outsiders eavesdropping. At the same time, the fact that their language is not read abroad is the source of loneliness to Japanese writers and scholars, who realize that the results of their diligent probings into, say, Anglo-Saxon land tenure or the poetry of Christina Rossetti are doomed to be unread even by specialists in the West.

The fact that the Japanese live on islands has naturally had more than a spiritual effect. The general defeated in one of the innumerable civil wars which beset Japan during her middle ages could not seek refuge abroad. There was in fact no escape, and the only alternative to humiliating capture was suicide. The Japanese lover was similarly unable to urge his sweetheart (as Don José urged Carmen) to begin a new life with him in America—or in China, for that matter. Nor was concealment possible within Japan, a country where privacy is unknown, and a reluctance to answer questions is in itself an occasion for suspicion. No matter how far the lovers could run there was always the sea around them to block a final escape, and in the end they often chose suicide. However, it is doubtful if the defeated general or the unhappy lovers would have wished to leave the Japanese islands, even had a boat been provided. So strong was the conviction that Japan was unique that the Japanese, though aware of course that other countries existed, tended to think of Japan as the whole world, and no amount of hardship could persuade them that they would be happier abroad.

The country with which the Japanese have had most to do since ancient times is China. They were in fact accustomed to thinking of China as the source of civilization, and were ready to consider and often to adopt any new Chinese philosophy, style of painting or medicine. The Japanese studied the Chinese classics with passionate devotion, composed works in the Chinese language, and sometimes even signed Chinese names to their writings. However, unlike certain other people within the orbit of Chinese civilization, the Japanese were proud of their nationality, and insisted on the fact that they were essentially unlike the Chinese. If obliged to admit their inferiority in material things, they could cling to the belief that they were spiritually superior to the Chinese, just as in a later day they would scorn the Americans for relying on material supremacy for success in war.

Moreover, no amount of Chinese influence could alter some of the basic features of Japanese life: the diet, with its dependence on fish and other products of the sea, and its insistence on undisguised, simple flavors, is very

4 *Commodore Perry (left) and his aide Captain Adams sketched by a Japanese artist at the time of their landing in 1853 to "open" Japan. The inscription above Perry reads literally "North America Republican Government Washington Fillmore Millard Commodore Matthew C. Perry Portrait."*

5 *Reading from left to right, the "civilized man," the "semi-civilized man" and the "un-civilized man," as depicted in a satirical work of 1871.*

21

different from the sauces and seasonings of Chinese cookery; the houses and household furnishings are quite different; and the clothes, though undoubtedly much influenced by the Chinese, developed in a Japanese manner. The Chinese from time to time imposed their dress and calendar on neighboring peoples, but the Japanese, thanks to their island situation, were never compelled to accept anything which did not appeal to their tastes.

Apart from two attempts by the Mongols to conquer the islands in 1274 and 1281 (the latter foiled by the celebrated "divine wind," or *kamikaze*), the Japanese never knew the threat of invasion. When European traders and missionaries arrived in the sixteenth and seventeenth centuries, the Japanese obliged them to conform to local regulations. Eventually, all Europeans but the Dutch were driven out by government edicts, and the Dutch were confined to a minuscule island in Nagasaki harbor, where they lived in a trading station as virtual prisoners.

Although the Japanese were extremely anxious to keep the foreigners under strict control, they remained highly receptive to foreign things and ideas. Many educated Japanese made the long journey to Nagasaki to learn what they could from the Dutch, at a time when no other source of information about the outside world was available. Dutch printed cottons, velvets and glass were highly prized even by ordinary townsmen.

Remoteness from the rest of the world, and the infrequency, over the centuries, of contacts with foreigners have made many Japanese timid and awkward in their personal dealings with foreigners ever since the country was opened in the 1860's. For the most part the Japanese, even many well-educated ones, feel uneasy and rather frightened before foreigners. The dignified old gentleman, seldom known to smile in his own country, will giggle nervously from the moment of his arrival abroad; cheerful conversation at a party of young intellectuals in Japan will become stiff and constrained with the appearance of a foreigner, however unassuming.

The Japanese uncertainty in dealing with foreigners is often repeated in their use of foreign things. Most modern houses, for example, have at least one Western-style room, furnished with overstuffed chairs, tables covered with doilies and ashtrays, and other appurtenances of modern life which one would not be surprised to find in a lower middle-class home in America or England, but which offer a dismal contrast to the serene, sparse elegance of the Japanese-style rooms next door. In part the ugliness of the furniture is the carpenters' fault: because they themselves never use overstuffed chairs and Western furniture in their own homes, they have no feeling for its comfort or beauty of line. But the Japanese, though blessed with a razor's edge perceptivity when dealing with anything native to the islands, often seem to lack the power of distinguishing the qualities of foreign things. In the *tokonoma* (the alcove in Japanese-style rooms for displaying hanging scrolls and flower arrangements), one may see yellow-haired dolls and rosy kewpie dolls, which seem charmingly exotic to the Japanese, and the gardens and parks often boast plaster replicas of "Mannikin Pis," the pride of Brussels.

It is not that the Japanese are ignorant of foreign countries. On the contrary, their bookshops are filled with translations of European novels, with learned volumes of statistics and analyses of economic and political developments abroad, and with commentaries on the great religious and philosophical works of the Western tradition. A foreign professor coming to teach at a Japanese university may be rather staggered at how well informed his undergraduates are in the writings of Kant, Hegel and Marx. Newspapers and magazines report events abroad in greater detail than local news, and politicans are more likely to express themselves on the policies of the American Secretary of State than on the advisability of building new roads and hospitals. But somehow the immense store of knowledge about the West which the educated Japanese possesses does not make him comfortable with it. He knows with one part of his mind, from having read Stendhal, Dostoevski and Hemingway, that people in the West experience much the same emotions he has himself, but he may tend to think of the non-Japanese as too cold and rationalistic.

Japan's long period of isolation accounts not only for a certain awkwardness in dealing with foreigners but for the unusual physical homogeneity of the population of Japan. To anyone who has grown up in the United States with its varied people, it seems curious that all of the names of students or soldiers or candidates for public office in Japan are of Japanese origin. Not only are all the names Japanese, but with the exception of the Ainu, an aboriginal people who survive today in small numbers mainly because they are the chief tourist attraction of the island of Hokkaido, it is virtually impossible to tell anything about the ancestry of a Japanese by his height, features or coloring. One sees a great variety of features, it is true, but they are not regional nor connected with the social class of a man's ancestors. The so-called aristocratic face and the so-called peasant face are likely to occur within the same family. Japanese have none of the regional peculiarities which distinguish, say, an Italian from Naples and one from Milan. The apparent homogeneity is all the more extraordinary in view of the fact that anthropologists generally agree that the Japanese are of mixed origin, blending a north Asian type with a southern "Malayan" type, and including also an admixture of the blood of the Ainu and other aboriginal peoples.

Regional accents and temperamental differences, however, are marked enough in Japan for people to think of a Tokyo man or a Kyushu man as being a special kind of Japanese. The open-hearted Tokyo man, the commercially-inclined Osaka man, and the conservative Kyoto man are indeed considered to be so different that people shake their heads when they hear of a marriage between, say, an Osaka man and a Tokyo girl.

It is not surprising that a Japanese who from his earliest childhood has associated only with people of Japanese ancestry, who never had a Negro or a blond schoolmate, nor, for that matter, a Chinese or a Filipino, should feel that Japanese and all foreigners are totally dissimilar. Even a well-educated Japanese may be rather surprised to discover that he and his Western friend get sick from eating the same bad food, or that if his nose runs on a cold day, the nose of the blondest young lady may also run. A Japanese's misconceptions of foreigners may lead him to glorify or to despise them, usually depending on their nationality. Europeans and Americans living in Japan come to accept as natural the exaggerated respect often shown them, and easily consent, for example, when their Japanese hosts urge them not to remove their shoes at the door, as if their footwear (unlike those of the Japanese) did not become muddy.

On the other hand, the Koreans, the largest group of foreigners in Japan today, enjoy no such privileged treatment. Many of them are illegal immigrants, and the average Japanese entertains such strong feelings of contempt and suspicion for them that any particularly unpleasant crime, desecration of public property or sinister traffic, is automatically blamed on the Koreans. For a long time the Chinese were held in almost equal contempt, but the military successes of the Communist regime have inspired greater respect for the Chinese.

The group which has suffered most in Japan from racial discrimination, however, is one indistinguishable from other Japanese in features and in speech. These are the *eta,* a pariah class of obscure origin, who have been condemned for many centuries to engage in occupations (such as the slaughter of animals or tanning) which other Japanese refused. It is now illegal to discriminate against the *eta,* but in practice they are compelled to live in ghettos, cannot marry outside their own group, and are refused employment by most private businesses. One might imagine that it would be perfectly simple for a member of the *eta* community to leave the special quarter where he lives and make a new life elsewhere, but in a country without privacy and where intimate questions are commonly put to casual acquaintances, it is almost impossible to change one's identity, and the *eta,* though better treated at present than in former days, still inspire disgust in many Japanese.

One other group of unfortunates who meet discrimination in Japan are the illegitimate offspring left behind by the Allied armies of occupation after the war. These children are likely to be taunted and bullied at school, and when they grow up may have trouble finding desirable jobs. However, the fact that for the first time in history large numbers of people with clearly un-Japanese features will be leading Japanese lives on the farms and in the factories and offices cannot but help shake the insularism which has been the blessing and curse of Japanese history.

6 *Land is so scarce that even steep hillsides along the coast are cultivated; on the Island of Awaji the rice terraces are built almost into the sea.*

7 *(Over) Mountains on three sides, the sea on the fourth hem in the Shonai Plain, one of the richest rice-growing regions of northern Honshu.*

8 *(Over) Rice grows almost everywhere in the Japanese islands, regardless of climate. In some regions two crops are harvested; in others, as here on the Izu Peninsula, one crop of rice follows one of wheat.*

9 *(Over) Most rice is grown in irrigated fields and cultivated by women as well as men.*

SUSUMU HIGUCHI: BUNGEI-SHUNJU

7

HIROSHI HAMAYA

8

EVANS: THREE LIONS

9   HIROSHI HAMAYA

10

HIROSHI HAMAYA

11

HIROSHI HAMAYA

Chapter II

THE OLD WAYS

10–11 In spring the women work five or six hours at a stretch planting rice seedlings in the icy marsh water—too cold for a man, they say. Modern improvements have not much affected the traditional agricultural ways.

JAPANESE SOCIETY is commonly said to be organized as a family system. Of course one might say that any society is a family system. In Japan, however, the family goes far beyond the relations of parents and children. It includes remote ancestors, distant relatives, and even people entirely unconnected by blood or marriage. Purely fictitious ties are honored with family names: a gang of hardened criminals, for example, will be headed by a "father" whose henchmen are expected as "children" to pay him appropriate respect. Japanese soldiers were formerly enjoined to look upon their company commander as their "father," their squad leader as their "mother" and senior privates as their "elder brother." A truly impressive political leader was often spoken of as being at once "a father and a mother" to the nation. Absurd as some of these relationships may seem to an outsider, they bear witness to how congenial the Japanese have found it to think in terms of a family.

The family system, though now so deeply rooted in Japan, was imported from China over the centuries as part of the larger body of Confucian thought. Indeed, the words most characteristic of the system were all borrowed from China—words like "filial piety" (*kô*), "duty" (*giri*), and "obligation" (*on*). Before the widespread adoption of these Chinese ideas, however, the family was by no means sacrosanct. Shinto has little to say about family obligations, and Buddhism actually praises men who abandon the world and their families to become priests. Confucian thought gained its supremacy as a guide to Japanese family conduct during the period of seclusion (from about 1630 to 1853), when the Tokugawa rulers of Japan deliberately fostered the teachings of the Chinese sage because they were believed to promote stability. Even after the Meiji Restoration of 1868 and the subsequent wholesale adoption of Western ideas, the rulers continued to insist that the Japanese be educated along traditional lines, and they proclaimed filial piety to be the source of all virtue. The state was often discussed as if it were a huge family headed by the emperor, and the identity of the loyalty due him and the filial piety due a father was frequently stressed. The Allied Occupation government of Japan rejected many of these beliefs as being "feudal," and instituted reforms in the educational system which were intended to weaken or destroy the family system. Nevertheless, the "feudal" ideas forbidden by the Allies and deplored by Japanese intellectuals continue to control most Japanese personal relationships today.

The simplest meaning of filial piety is the proper behavior expected of a child in return for his parents' kindnesses, especially for the supreme kindness of having given him life. Japanese elementary school children were formerly taught to show their parents extreme respect: "You must never stretch out your legs in the direction of your parents. When somebody talks about your parents you must sit up straight and listen, even if it means getting up out of bed." Even today in old-fashioned households the child is expected to serve his parents, and especially his father. The father's least word is a command, and the child must obey unquestioningly, long after he is grown up himself. One ancient Chinese model of filial piety was a man who dressed as an infant at the age of sixty and played with toys so that his eighty-year-old parents might not feel old.

The child is also expected to enhance the family prestige by becoming successful. Whether successful or not, however, he is expected to look after his parents—probably his greatest obligation. Finally, he must continue the family line by producing children of his own.

This system may arouse either the envy or distress of non-Japanese. By ruling out the preferences of the individual and substituting instead as its goal the stability of the family, the system solved many problems now faced by Western society. A Japanese traveling abroad, for example, is often shocked by the treatment of old people—the lonely old men in the parks, the lonely old women eating in cheap restaurants, the signs that children have considered that by giving their parents an allowance, they were doing all that was necessary. Lonely old people are much rarer in Japan than in the West. Virtually everyone marries, and if the marriage is not blessed with children, adoptions are easily arranged. The Japanese can be sure that, barring some disaster, his children will take care of him when he is old. This assumes a good deal of sacrifice on the part of the children, particularly in the cramped quarters of a Japanese house, but few refuse to make the sacrifice. In the country especially a household is likely to consist of three generations, and the grandmother controls the purse strings. A Japanese may therefore anticipate the coming of old age with less trepidation than most of his contemporaries in the West, and he knows that after death his children and distant descendants will honor his memory.

Yet despite the promise of a secure old age and the kind of immortality

12 Women harvesting rice in Yamagata wear masks to ward off insects and protect their faces from the sun. Originally, it is said, these also shielded them from the ogling of overseers.

13 Most rice is threshed by machine; it is done by hand only in remote districts.

14 In the daily market at Wajima, a fishing village on the northwest coast, the women sell bamboo shoots, lotus roots and yams.

12

13   ORLANDO: THREE LIONS

14   HIROSHI HAMAYA

HIROSHI HAMAYA

15   ORLANDO: THREE LIONS

ORLANDO: THREE LIONS

16

17   KEN HEYMAN: RAPHO GUILLUMETTE

afforded by ancestor worship, not all Japanese are content with the family system. To the degree that a Japanese has been affected by Western ideas of individuality and personality, he will find the rigid existing order to be painfully constricting. He may revolt in many ways. He may decide to build a home of his own away from his parents; he may make a love marriage instead of accepting the bride selected by his parents; or he may choose a profession quite out of keeping with family traditions. Some Japanese, particularly in Tokyo, are able to break so far away from their filial duties that they lead lives virtually indistinguishable from those of New Yorkers or Londoners. The majority, however, continue to live (to a greater or lesser extent) within the framework of the family system.

The Japanese reared under this system is aware from his earliest childhood of his place in life. If he is a younger son, for example, he learns to call his elder brother not by his name but by the words "elder brother," and learns to accept as inevitable the fact that the elder son, as the heir to the family, will receive preferential treatment in everything, even being allowed to share with the father in delicacies untasted by the rest of the family. If he is an elder son he takes such privileges as his due, knowing at the same time that his will be the heavier responsibilities in the future. If the child is a daughter, she knows that her life will be one of waiting on men—her father, her brothers, her husband, and her own sons. Her greatest virtue is therefore submissiveness, and she is trained to have no "selfish" desires. Eventually, as a mother-in-law, she will at last have someone she herself can bully. Numerous novels tell of the cruel treatment traditionally visited on daughters-in-law and step-children by Japanese women. This may be a kind of compensation exacted for the long years of patient suffering.

The family system and the self-sacrifice it requires have made Japanese women into the models of femininity so praised by the rest of the world. The husband's duty to his family is to marry a wife chosen for him, even if he does not love her, and to beget children. If he complies with these two rules he may have as many extramarital connections as he pleases, and even boast of them before his wife. He assumes that his wife will tolerate his lapses from fidelity and all lesser discourtesies. If he returns at midnight after carousing with his friends, he does not feel it necessary to apologize for having missed dinner. Far from it, he may be annoyed if a hot meal is not waiting for him even at that hour. His wife may be dressed in threadbare clothes, and wintry gales may be whistling through broken window-panes, but the husband will not hesitate to spend the evening at a bar drinking liquor which costs far more than the needed clothes for his wife or a new window.

If the husband is rich enough he may keep one or more mistresses under the same roof with his wife. The only proper behavior for a wife under these circumstances is to bear everything patiently. She must never appear jealous, and must not complain. If she cheerfully endures the worst that her husband can do, she is universally praised.

Of course, not all husbands, even of the traditional variety, behave so outrageously, and "enlightened" husbands, whose attitudes are similar to those of men in Western countries, are increasing. However, a wife in a traditional household must always be prepared to accept abuse without a murmur. Only in the large cities is divorce socially acceptable as a woman's defense against a brutal husband; elsewhere, women are still expected to endure anything in the interests of the family.

Under the family system, the desirability of having children does not stem from the fact that they make a house a home, or that they add joy to the lives of the parents; sons are necessary to carry on the family line and to pray for the spirits of their ancestors. If, therefore, a couple is childless, a son must be adopted. If parents have an only daughter, they will often choose a suitable young man, give him an education, train him in the family business, and then marry their daughter to him. The boy will take his wife's surname after the wedding ceremony. It sometimes happens when the sons of a family die without heirs that a married daughter is obliged to remarry her husband, with the husband assuming her maiden name at the second ceremony.

In addition to families which live under one roof and resemble families elsewhere, Japan has many varieties of fictitious families. Most of the traditional arts, including Japanese dance, the Nô, flower arrangement, and the different schools of singing to *samisen* accompaniment are organized as families. Each school has a "head of the family" (*iemoto*), who rules the hundreds or even thousands of members of his clan with paternal despotism. When a student has mastered the dance, or whatever art he is learning, he is officially given the surname of the "head of the family" and a personal name derived from his own teacher's. By this act he becomes a full-fledged member of the family, and is expected, among other things, to visit the graves of his new ancestors at the appropriate times. He will henceforth refer to the other members of the school as his "family."

The head of the family takes his responsibilities seriously, and acts with the mixture of sternness and compassion expected of a real father. The head of the Ichikawa acting family, for example, is reported to have remarked after a troupe of young actresses was honored with the Ichikawa name, "I am delighted to have acquired seventeen daughters all at once, but when I think that in another five or six years' time I will be giving them away in marriage, I can see that being a father will be quite an expensive proposition, no matter how small a wedding present I offer each."

The position of head of the family is usually transmitted directly from father to son. It sometimes happens, of course, that the son of a great dancer or actor does not inherit his father's talents. He will nevertheless in most cases

18 A Japanese house uses wood in every shape—latticework sidings, the frames of shoji screens, balcony railings, washtubs, flower boxes. Izu.

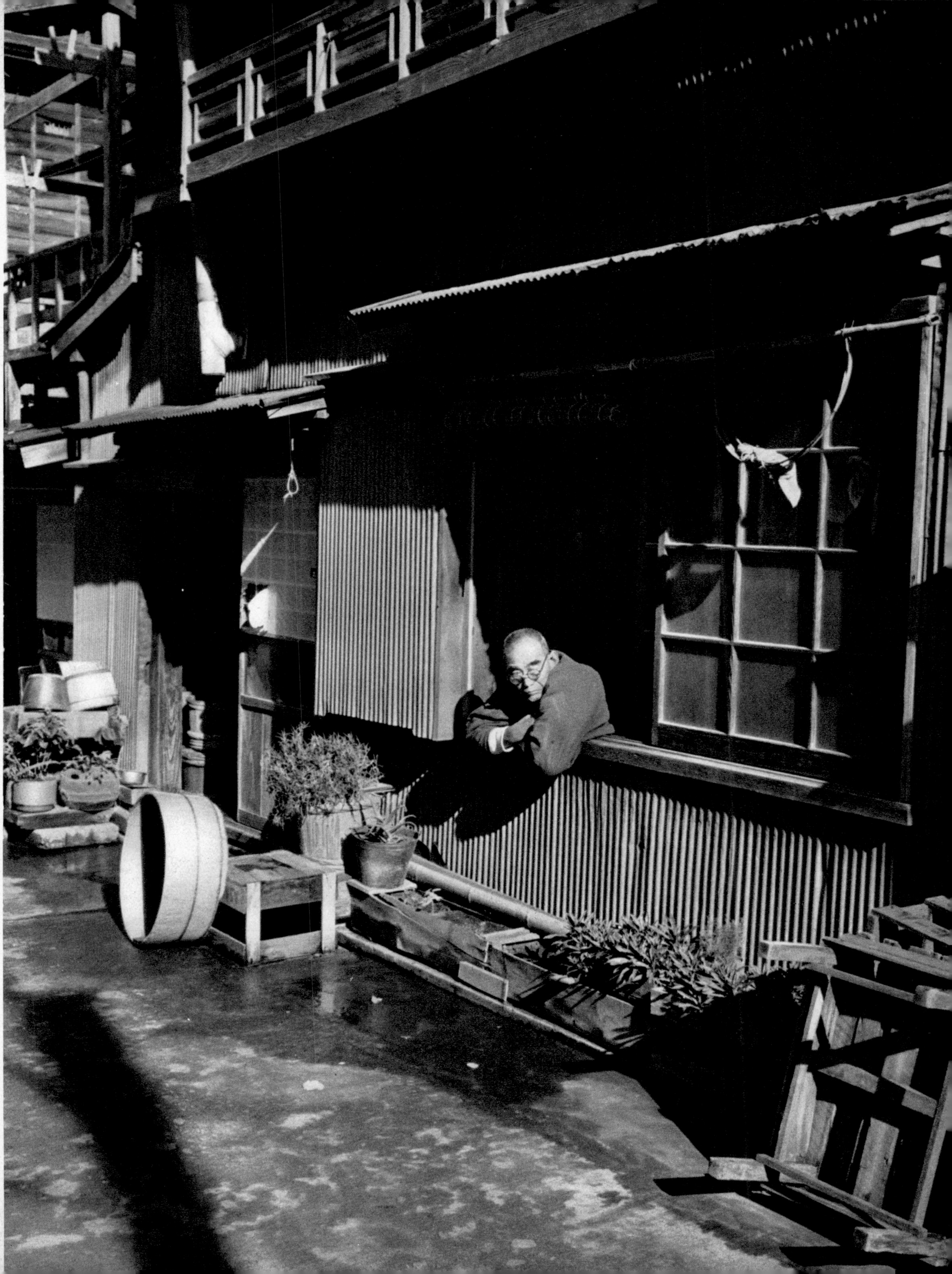

Ken Heyman: Rapho Guillumette

19

20

TAKENORI TANUMA: CHUOKORON-SHA

HIROSHI HAMAYA

succeed to the headship though occasionally a boy from a different "family" will be adopted and trained to be the successor. Adoption, indeed, has been an indispensable factor in the preservation of the family system in all forms of the arts.

Even in the world of scholarship we can see the family pattern. A professor often acts like a father to his disciples, arranging their marriages (woe betide a disciple who marries without his permission!) and choosing his most promising student for his own daughter. The head of a family of dancers will honor the recital of one of his "children" with his presence or performance; a professor will write a preface for his "child's" book.

When the family system is applied to the arts, it offers performers distinct advantages. The "child" not only benefits from the experience and skills of his teacher, but is protected by him from unemployment. He is helped by the head of the family to found a branch of the school, and the head sees to it, moreover, that branches are geographically distributed in such a manner that fellow "children" do not interfere with one another's livelihoods. The head also transmits secrets of his profession to some of his disciples, thereby enabling them to become masters themselves.

Such control over the different arts has undoubtedly helped to preserve a high level of competence. Nevertheless, the Japanese have become increasingly impatient with this "feudal" system, particularly since the non-traditional arts (such as ballet, piano and modern theater) are not organized paternalistically. They complain, for example, that even outstanding talent is not enough to permit a young man or woman to become a recognized dancer (or flower arranger, or musical performer). A girl who would like to make a career as a dancer, for example, must pay an exorbitant fee to the head of the family when she takes his name and must continue to contribute to his support. She is not free to develop as her talents lead her; she must dance in exact conformity to the family dictates or risk being stricken from the family ranks. (One dancer who performed to the accompaniment of Western music was removed from the family rolls immediately.) The fact that the head of the school may be inferior as an artist to some of his "children" makes such restrictions all the more irksome.

There is usually no choice but to comply, for in most of the traditional arts it is impossible to perform in public unless one belongs to a family. Each of the arts is dominated by two or three families. In the puppet theater, for example, all the operators of puppets have for surnames either Yoshida or Kiritake; the chanters are all either Takemoto or Toyotake; and the players of the *samisen,* the instrument which accompanies the performances, all bear one of three surnames. Not only is the player restricted to a few "families," but his artistic name must also be inherited from some illustrious predecessor. The "naming" ceremony is an important moment in any performer's life.

19–20 *Every January 14th the children of Tokamachi, a village in the heart of the Japanese "Snow Country," build little igloos where they sing songs and prepare feasts, a relic of ancient purification rites.*

One effect of the family system, whether in real or fictitious families, is to limit severely and sometimes to extinguish individuality. In theory the young dancer first imitates exactly his teacher's every movement, but later, when a mature artist, demonstrates his individual excellence. In practice, however, a constant bowing to parental authority often ends by weakening the independence and creativeness of the "child," and when he himself becomes a "parent" he will insist on the old ways rather than attempt innovations. Takeyoshi Kawashima, a leading Japanese sociologist, has blamed on this paternalism "the fact that the general tendency or even desire of the vast majority of Japanese is to have no sense of being independent entities in the face of superior force or authority, but instead to surrender themselves unconditionally, with an awareness only of their obedience." If this is true, the family system may be credited with making the Japanese orderly, peaceable and submissive (at least within their families), but it has also been responsible for their feeble resistance to tyrants. The strength of the Japanese army formerly came from farm boys reared within the strictest families, because they were ready to execute any order unquestioningly. The same kind of family training even today could produce blind adherents of either the extreme right or left.

The family system is hierarchical, as indeed is the whole of Japanese society. The father stands at the top of the hierarchy, the eldest son comes next, and succeeding sons are often numbered for convenience: "Health Two," "Obedience Three," and so on. Even if no numbers are attached, the order in the hierarchy of any "family" is known. "I am the sixth best *kyogen* actor in Osaka," or "He is the fourth best Japanese violinist in the United States" are statements typical of a people acutely aware of rank and precedence. The Japanese child is taught to distinguish the words he may properly say to a younger brother and those he must use to his parents or a stranger. This is not merely a matter of adding a word like "sir" to a sentence, but in many cases involves an entirely separate vocabulary. The simple word "is," for example, can take as different forms as *da* and *de gozaimasu*. There is a rich variety of honorifics and of humble words, and the misuse of them can make any sentence, even something like "This is my hat," seem excessively polite or grossly rude. Often the content of an utterance is of less importance than its level of politeness. When strangers meet they at first spar gingerly in high honorifics, but as questions reveal their respective positions in the hierarchy, one will switch to a familiar, condescending language and the other to polite verb endings. This is as true of leaders of progressive thought as of old gentlemen in the country. If, for example, a university teacher tries to prove how democratic he is by addressing his students with polite language, he will probably succeed only in bewildering or even embarrassing them. On the other hand, if he forgets to use honorifics when speaking to an older colleague, he will be considered highly impertinent.

21 *At the "snow market" in Tokamachi farmers sell the products of their winter work— straw raincoats, buckets, winnows, snow-shoes.*

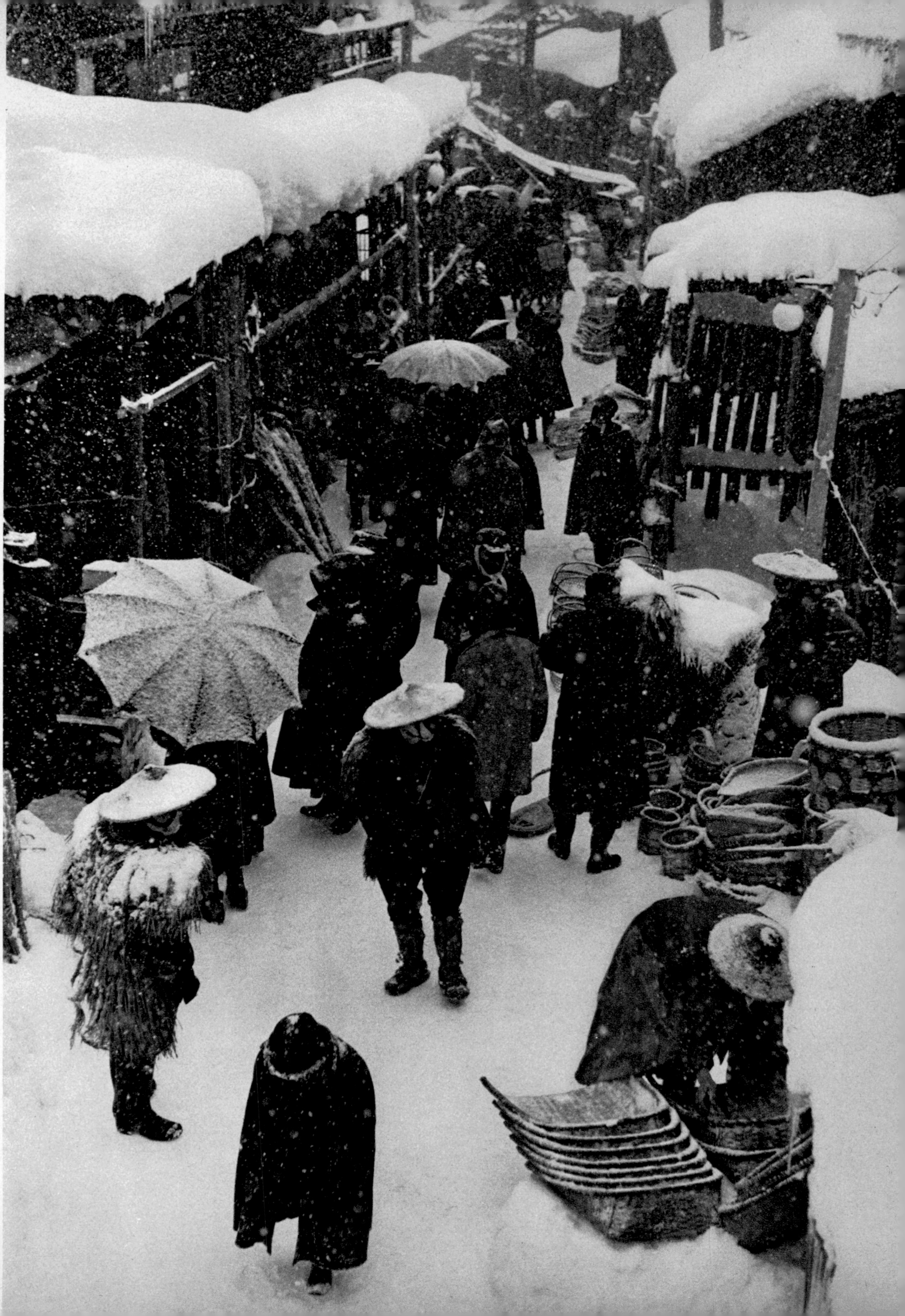

HIROSHI HAMAYA

The use of honorifics is accentuated by bows, smiles, and other gestures, all of which make it exceedingly apparent when two people are conversing what their relative positions are in the hierarchy. The shift from one level to another can be almost instantaneous. The priest deferentially bowing to visitors who come to his temple may suddenly bark out a peremptory command to a temple servant, and as quickly shift to soft honorifics again. To talk humbly to a servant would not really be humble or polite, even for a priest, but would make him seem rather ridiculous.

22 The children of Tokamachi trudge off to the January 14th festival in their new straw raincoats and snow-shoes.

Because each person knows his place and how he must talk to others, social intercourse is often smoother than in less rigidly organized societies. There is none of the aggressive determination of the American elevator boy or taxi-driver to prove that he is just as good as his passengers, nor the uncertainties of who gets seated at the captain's table on a ship. When a group of people go together into a dining room, they generally know exactly where to sit—who will be closest to the flower arrangement and who must be content with a place near the door. An attempt to make things more democratic by substituting a round table or the like will probably cause the guests to run round and round the table, unhappy not to know their place.

Even in a hierarchical society, however, people sometimes like to associate without the necessity of obeying complicated rules of etiquette and using prescribed honorifics. Saké makes this possible. In other countries liquor is a pleasant adjunct to life, but in Japan it is the indispensable element which enables, say, the employees of a company to relax and become friendly even with superiors without remembering to address them always as "Mr. Assistant Department Director," or "Mr. Supervisor of the Bureau." The formal relations are immediately restored when the effects of the liquor have worn off, and drinking companions are seldom friends in sober hours.

Friends seem less important to the Japanese than they are to most other peoples. A man may have numerous drinking pals and lady friends, but in moments of crisis he usually turns to his family rather than to friends. Japanese are surprised when they visit the United States to hear how often the word "friendship" is used, and with what emphasis. In Japan friends are for the most part former classmates. The Japanese have unbounded nostalgia for old acquaintances, and even kindergarten classes regularly hold reunions twenty or thirty years after graduation. Grown men can grow maudlin about events which took place when they were seven or eight years old. But it is extremely difficult to make close friends with anyone who was not a schoolmate. Fellow students at an elementary school are equals and can therefore become friends, but as a Japanese grows older the sense of hierarchy interferes with his associations. For some Japanese it is easier to make friends with foreigners than with fellow countrymen, because foreigners stand outside the Japanese hierarchy.

Because of the family system, the fewness of friends does not matter as much to the Japanese as it would to Americans. As this system is weakened, however, the Japanese will taste more of the pleasure of free association and the pangs of solitude, and friends will be as essential as elsewhere. The family system has successfully dealt with most problems likely to arise in communal living and has made for a stable society. It has also accounted for much that is praiseworthy in the arts, though Japanese today are more apt to point out its failings. It has functioned most smoothly when unchallenged by rival ideas; the discovery by Japanese students of the West of the rights of the individual has especially shaken the old system.

The Japan which Commodore Perry visited in 1853 was not a happy country—hunger, disease, infanticide and all the ills attendant on an absolute dictatorship made life far worse for the Japanese than it is today. Nevertheless, numerous early visitors testified that the Japanese were an amiable, courteous and well-disciplined people, thanks to the pervasive influence of the Confucian teachings. Each Western idea that has gained currency in Japan has made the Japanese a little less like their tractable ancestors. But, despite the changes, they still have much in common, a fact which should suggest how deeply rooted the old ways were.

23 A Japanese farm kitchen contains not only pots and pans but a straw winnow on the wall, and teacups on a tray for men in the fields.

24 In a prosperous farmhouse near Hiroshima the successful planting of the rice is celebrated with good cheer and feasting.

ORLANDO: THREE LIONS

23

24

HIDEO HAGA: CHUOKORON-SHA

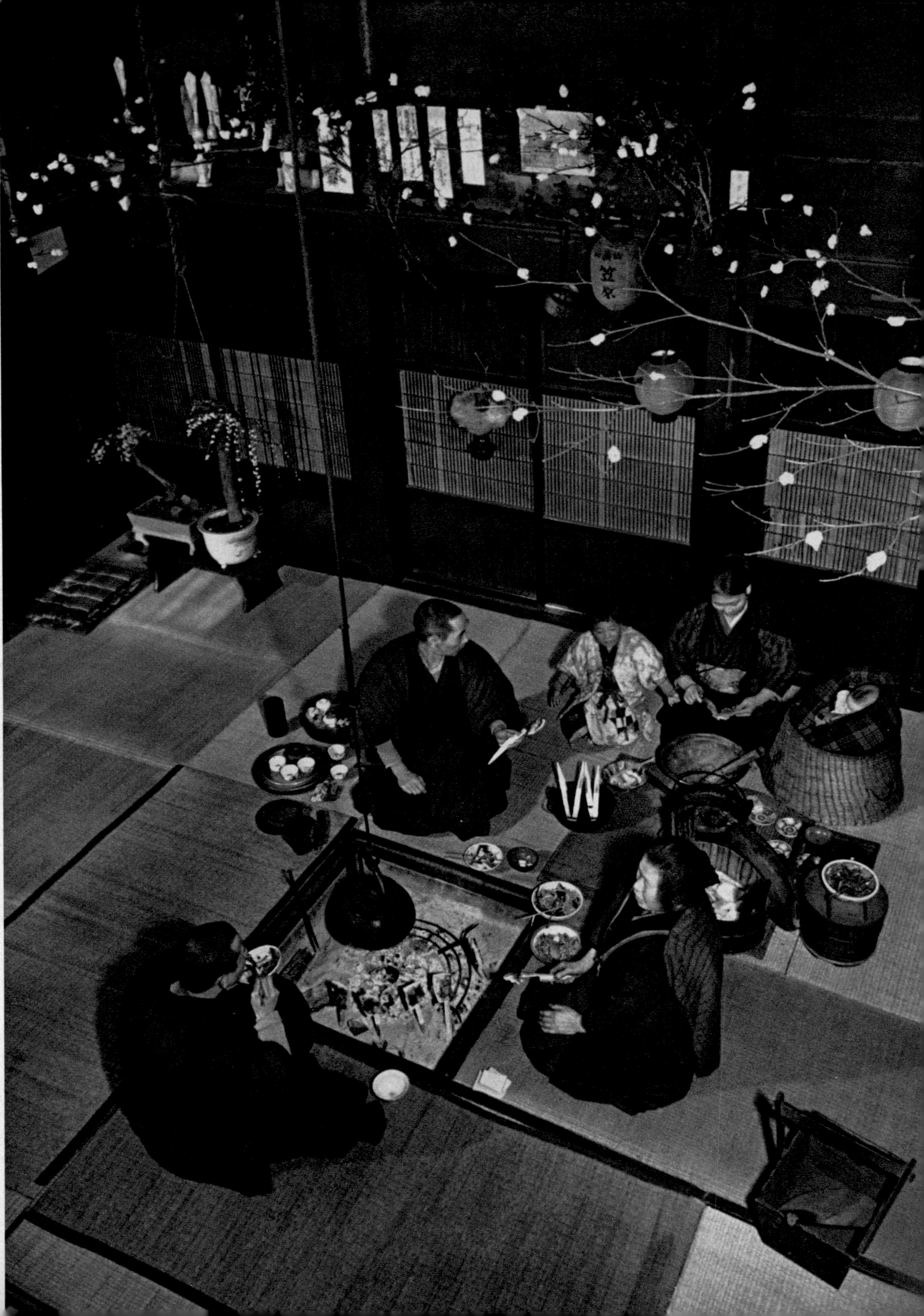

Hiroshi Hamaya

THE NEW WAYS

THE TIDE of Western influence which swept over Japan in the 1870's all but engulfed the Japanese. The advanced thinkers proclaimed the superiority of Western civilization, and the Emperor himself, in the oath he took on assuming office, declared that during his reign knowledge would be sought throughout the world in order to promote the welfare of the nation. In a remarkably short time the Japanese were studying not only Western techniques—at which they quickly showed themselves adept—but the political institutions and eventually the literature of Europe and America. Some conservatives had their doubts about the propriety of adopting "barbarian learning," but most men unhesitatingly bowed before the new gods. One important official went so far as to suggest that the Japanese language ought to be abolished altogether in favor of English. Another writer, deeply impressed by the achievements of the West, argued that the Japanese were physically and mentally inferior to Occidental peoples, and recommended as a remedy that Japanese men divorce their wives and marry Western females of superior physique and intellect. Even people unable to accept such drastic suggestions eagerly followed the new modes. Here is a satiric description of a dandy of 1871:

"A man about thirty-five, rather swarthy it is true, but of clear complexion, thanks apparently to the daily use of soap, which purges all impurities. His hair is long and flowing in the foreign style. Naturally enough, he uses that scent called eau de Cologne to give a sheen to his locks. He wears a padded silken kimono beneath which a calico undergarment is visible. By his side is his Western-style umbrella, covered in gingham. From time to time (with a painfully contrived gesture) he removes a cheap watch from his sleeve and consults the time."

In every direction the Japanese were busily making themselves European as rapidly as possible, usually showing no concern for the preservation of their own traditions. In order to raise funds for modern improvements, some of the great treasures of Japanese art were offered for sale to foreigners, and monuments of Japanese architecture were threatened by the demon progress. A guidebook to the architectural beauties of Kyoto published in 1885, for example, reserved its highest praise for a factory, a high school and a hall of industrial arts, all in the fashionable Western style. The newly introduced civilization and its appurtenances came to take precedence over the old refinements. The Emperor and Empress were photographed in Western dress—the Emperor in a military uniform and the Empress in crinolines—and the high society of the 1880's flocked at night to the Rokumei Hall in Tokyo, a Victorian-style building to demonstrate to foreigners their mastery of the waltz.

In literature and arts the impact was no less overwhelming. By 1905, less than forty years after the accession of the Emperor Meiji opened the new era, there were young men, even in the remote villages, who had read Ibsen, could quote the Bible or discuss Greek mythology, play Wagner and Mendelssohn on the harmonium, and were beginning to interest themselves in anarchist or socialist thought. Painting in oils became the chosen medium of most of the young artists. Kabuki actors tried to incorporate Western ideas in their productions, and offstage some chose to attire themselves in frock coats and bowler hats purchased at stylish shops in Yokohama.

The Russo-Japanese War raised Japan to the status of a world power. A country where less than forty years before men had fought in corded armor defeated a modern European power both on land and on the sea. In parts of the world the Japanese came to enjoy legal status as Europeans, in contrast to persons from elsewhere in Asia. Indeed, it seemed to some observers as if soon nothing would be left of traditional Japan. They reckoned without the amazing ability of the Japanese to retain the things of the past.

Japan ist a museum of the fads of the past thousand years, mellowed and given dignity by the years. The popular songs of the Chinese court of the eighth century are today the stately ceremonial music of the Japanese court; a nineteenth-century Gothic revival church is classed as a national treasure along with masterpieces of traditional Buddhist architecture. Chinese books long since vanished in China have been discovered in Japan, and future students of Edwardian lampshades and tablecloths may have to journey to Japan for their research materials. Again and again it has been predicted that a traditional Japanese art is about to perish, but when the last-known practitioner dies someone else generally appears to carry on his work—whether it is carving heads for the puppet theater or making artificial flowers for some ancient ceremony.

The changes which took place in the years preceding the Russo-Japanese War were enormous, but they have been dwarfed by even more startling changes in later years, particularly since 1945. The most traditional institutions have been affected: pilgrims still trudge their weary way around the island of Shikoku

26 *One of Tokyo's most impressive "sights" is the massive moat surrounding the Imperial Palace. The buildings in the background formerly housed the headquarters of the Allied Occupation force.*

27 *The modern architecture of a Tokyo department store—no less than the poster of Mlle Brigitte Bardot—is in the "international style."*

28 *(Over) Osaka, second largest city in Japan, has been famous for centuries not only for its commercial enterprise but its variety of restaurants and entertainment.*

29 *(Over) The pleasure of being part of a crowd is one of the great attractions of Tokyo for country-dwellers.*

26

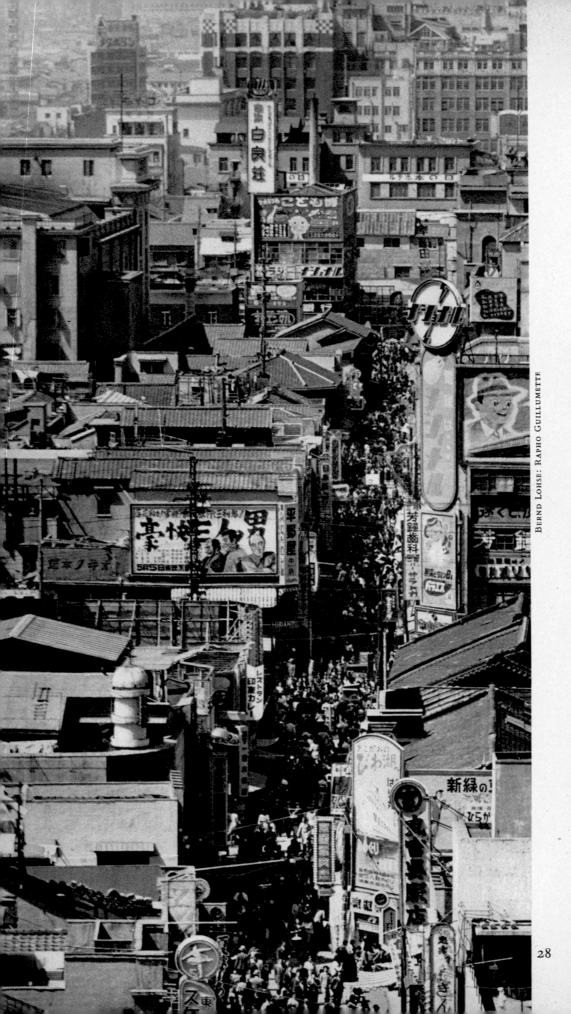

28

29

MARC RIBOUD: MAGNUM

30

31

to worship at each of the eighty-eight holy sites, but they may wear over the customary pilgrim's garb a vinyl raincoat to protect them from the elements. The visitor to a tea ceremony performed by one of the more up-to-date schools may be startled to discover that his tea has been whipped with an electric mixer. And a show of modern flower arrangements is likely to offer no flowers at all or only conspicuously foreign ones, such as orchids or zinnias. Yet in a sense what is most interesting is not the vinyl raincoat, the electric mixer and the zinnias, but the fact that pilgrims, tea masters and flower arrangers are still recognized as members of Japanese society.

Japan today is a modern country from which the past has not been dislodged. In the street next to a glass-walled factory may stand houses which would not much surprise a Japanese born centuries ago; in the same block with the movie house and the strip-tease palace may be a theater where eighteenth-century puppet plays are performed with scrupulous fidelity to the original texts. From a modern street in Tokyo, lined with garish advertisements and pinball parlors, we may pass into a Japanese restaurant hardly different from one built a hundred years ago. The floor is covered with the simple elegance of *tatami* matting, and there is a *tokonoma* graced by a painting and a flower arrangement. A low lacquer table is the only article of furniture. A kimono-clad waitress serves the meal, carefully watching the guest's saké cup lest it become empty. The meal itself will probably be much the same as a hundred years ago.

We may think in leaving the street crowded with busses, bicycles and three-wheeled trucks for the restaurant that we have journeyed from the present to the past, but this is a mistake. The restaurant is not a museum; it is an expression of contemporary preference. Most Japanese today, even the young rebels against tradition, feel happier eating a meal in such surroundings than in a conventional Western-style restaurant with chairs and tables disposed in one large room. Some Japanese have attempted to lead almost entirely Western lives. They live in modern apartments in Tokyo which afford them a luxury unknown elsewhere in Japan: privacy. The radicals among them relate (not without a touch of pride) that they have never worn a kimono or even that they dislike the taste of rice. Such extremists, however, are few and, if past example can serve as a guide, most of them by the time they are thirty-five or forty will discover the pleasures of the traditional Japanese ways.

The most typical style of living, in the cities at least, is what the Japanese themselves call "a compromise between East and West." This compromise does not always embody the best features of both worlds, but in principle the convenience of Western things is blended with the comfortable familiarity of old Japan. In a well-to-do household, for example, callers are entertained with coffee and cake in a reception room where stiffly arranged chairs and a heavily draped table make relaxation difficult. The real friends of the family are welcomed in a Japanese-style room and may be invited to change from their busi-

30 *In Tokyo, countless back streets lined with bars come to life every night.*

31 *Public telephones, seen everywhere along the streets in the big cities, afford no privacy, though traffic noises help.*

ness suits to kimonos. The modern host may be a connoisseur of cheeses and European wines, but he is no less expert in judging a piece of salted fish or a Japanese pickle. The modern hostess in her Paris-inspired gown will probably sit in Japanese fashion in a corner of the room and not contibute a word.

In the small towns and villages, of course, much less of the West has found its way into daily life. A farmer may have abandoned Japanese clothes in favor of trousers and a shirt, and he may ride a bicycle (or even a motorcycle) to his fields, but his house, his food, and his relations with his neighbors will probably be modelled on those of his grandfather before him. His responsibilities under the family system dominate his daily life, and the way he votes in an election is likely to depend more on such ties than on calculations of self-interest. Yet even though the farmer's house itself shows few signs, except for the electric lights, of the tremendous changes of the past half-century, the signs will be there: in the entrance where visitors and family remove their footgear, shoes of shiny plastic may be ranged next to straw sandals and wooden clogs, and a radio may be heard sending forth a Mozart violin concerto.

Such a combination of disparate elements has made many foreign visitors, disappointed that not all the women wear kimonos, offer the invariable advice that the Japanese should stick to their own things. They do not realize that in fact the Japanese are probably unique in their attachment to the costumes and other institutions of the past. People in the West tend to think of the things of the past as belonging to the past, and do not normally wear eighteenth-century clothes, write with a quill or drink mead. A Japanese woman in a kimono is in effect wearing an eighteenth-century costume, one intended for sitting on the floor rather than on a chair. On the other hand, a Japanese man in a business suit will gladly go to a restaurant where he must sit in a manner certain to take the crease out of his trousers. The foreigner who urges Japanese women to wear kimonos exclusively should instead marvel at their continued devotion to a costume which is expensive, complicated to put on, unbearably hot in summer, constricting to the wearer's movements, and which must be completely unsewn and resewn every time it is washed. If the Japanese today were more "logical" in their tastes, they would have long since adopted the kind of dress which goes most conveniently with busses and servant shortages.

The various conflicts and compromises between old and new which are visible everywhere in Japan today have their parallels in the minds and emotions of the Japanese. In the early nineteenth century, when Western cannons and other mechanical devices first interested the Japanese, a leading thinker advocated "Western techniques and Eastern morality," a formula which was intended to preserve the essence of the traditional society while borrowing the practical benefits of foreign science. This may sound feasible: why shouldn't the man who learned Western mathematics and chemistry also be a Confucian scholar? Some men in fact attempted to combine the two systems of thought, but they discovered that it took all of their time to learn science, and that they could not spend long hours perusing the Confucian classics. Moreover, the general contempt for practical, mechanical matters displayed by the old scholars was distasteful to men who were devoting their energies to a painful acquisition of such knowledge. Their whole view of the world was inevitably affected by new studies which could not simply be relegated to the domain of "techniques." Despite the efforts of the government to preserve and encourage the traditional learning, the men who sought practical knowledge from foreign countries generally ended up by drinking deeply in the spiritual culture as well.

The Japanese discovered, for example, the glories of Western literature, and the trickle of translations which began in the 1870's gradually swelled to a torrent. Almost every important work of European or American literature has been rendered into Japanese, sometimes in three or four different versions. It is said that a man who knew no foreign language could read more of the world's literature in Japanese than in any other tongue. The fondness for Western novels was not simply based on curiosity about what topics foreigners privately discussed or how they made love. It came from the realization that a book by an Englishman or a Russian could tell them much about themselves. The Japanese reader found the expression of the emotions unlike the kind with which he was familiar—when, for instance, a hero like Werther professed to be the "slave" of his beloved, or when another kind of hero declared his intention of "conquering" Nature. Yet even if a Japanese could not quite share such emotions, much of these novels moved him in ways that traditional Japanese literature did not. Imitation of foreign models was to bring about a liberation from the old conventions.

One of the leading figures in the formation of modern Japanese literature was Mori Ogai (1862–1922), a man born into a strict samurai family and educated as a boy in accordance with Confucian principles. After the Meiji Restoration of 1868 and the subsequent breakup of the old feudal system, Mori's father took the boy to Tokyo to learn German, as part of his preparation for becoming a physician. From 1884 to 1888 Mori studied medicine in Germany. While he was there he also read European literature and philosophy, and in 1889 published a volume of translations of German poetry. In the following year he wrote an original short story describing the unhappy attachment between a Japanese student in Berlin and a German dancing girl. Mori himself called the story an "I novel," and the strongly autobiographical tone shows how far European example had removed him from the tradition of impersonality in Japanese fiction. One of his later books entitled *Vita Sexualis* shocked people by the frankness with which he discussed his personal life.

But the traditional literary values, which Mori had so long implicitly denied, came to the surface again in his writings when he learned in 1912 that General Nogi (the hero of the Russo-Japanese War) and his wife had committed suicide following the death of the late Emperor Meiji. This dramatic gesture, the product of the same Confucian training which Mori himself had once known, moved him so deeply that from then on he wrote only novels exalting the old morality.

Mori Ogai was unusual in that he broke away from the traditional ways in both scientific and humanistic learning. To the end of his career as a physician—he eventually rose to be Surgeon General of the Japanese Army—he continued to stand for Western techniques, but in matters of the spirit he felt increasingly the pull of the past. Yet even when he was writing about some samurai of a hundred years before who had chosen to follow the code of honor of his ancestors, Mori could not help incorporating modern psychological insights, and his style was the new one which he himself had perfected. In other words, he could return to the past only with a consciousness of the present.

An outspoken break with the past followed by a gradual reconciliation with some of its ideals and comforts (without, however, approximating a pre-Western Japanese) has become so familiar a cycle that one is tempted to smile at present-day rebels and predict that presently they too will succumb to the charms of the past. Certainly there lingers in almost any young man, no matter how much he may deny that he feels specifically Japanese, a receptivity to the past which, for example, makes the tears come to his eyes when he sees a film about the traditional heroes, or which makes him laugh with delight at some of the old picaresque tales. But nobody knows until it actually happens that this cycle of change will take place, and perhaps with the rebels of today it never will. One would not find a very sympathetic audience if one told a group of angry young men that before long they would be sure to appreciate better the family system and all the rest of the traditional morality.

There have been protesting intellectuals in Japan almost since the first contacts with Western ideas. Some of them agitated for political reforms, others expressed their dislike for conventionality by wearing outlandish garb or by deliberate eccentricities. But they knew that there were certain bounds they could not overstep with impunity: some who ventured too far to the left died in prison, and others were forced to recant or to be silent. During the war even completely innocuous literature was frowned on if it did not seem to promote the resolute austerity expected of Japanese, and anything (even in the ancient classics) which failed to show the proper respect for the Imperial Family was ruthlessly expunged. With the defeat came the changes which have enabled the Japanese today to question the very nature of their society. A magazine editor wrote in May, 1946, "Speech is freer than it ever has been. No one now need fear persecution, no matter how radical his views may be. This is an absolutely unprecedented atmosphere for political activity and for the growth of intellectual ideas in Japan." Ironically enough, the pages of the same magazine were soon to be filled with the most bitter attacks on the Americans who had brought this new freedom to Japan. Anyone or anything standing in a position of

32   *Forests of television antennae rise over the low roofs of Tokyo.*

33   *Behind the houses in a poor district of Tokyo is a woman's world—washing, children, and perhaps a little garden.*

32

33

34

authority became a target for demonstrations and abuse. When the Emperor visited Kyoto University, where students half a dozen years before had bowed in worship to him, his car was surrounded by a mob of jeering young men. To Americans who remembered how their friends attended newsreel theaters in the thirties for the express purpose of booing President Roosevelt, this incident seemed regrettable but not unduly alarming, but to Japanese brought up under the old system it seemed that the world had turned topsy-turvy.

If the Emperor, who stood at the very apex of the Japanese family system, could be attacked with impunity, it naturally followed that lesser members of the system would suffer. One novelist made his reputation by writing wildly popular stories in which sons assault their fathers, younger brothers trade girl friends with elder brothers, and students knock their teachers to the ground with one well-placed uppercut. The threat to the old order has been bitterly resented by parents—even those not manhandled by their children. They complain that children no longer show respect to their elders and that juvenile delinquency has increased as a result. They are not the first to complain in these terms. As early as 1895 Lafcadio Hearn, reflecting on the changes which Western ideas had brought to Japan, remarked, "The old moral ideas of Japan were at least quite as noble as our own; and men could really live up to them in the quiet beneficial times of patriarchal government. Untruthfulness, dishonesty, and brutal crime were rarer than now, as official statistics show; the percentage of crime having been for some years steadily on the increase."

The fact would seem to be that any step in the direction of freedom, of dignity of the individual or expression of personal feelings is bound to come in conflict with a system which taught that the highest good was to kill all consciousness of the self and to perform one's allotted tasks faithfully in slavish silence. The first word of protest uttered by a young man will be interpreted as gross insubordination by his elders, and they are in a sense right, for under the old system there was no room for anything but unquestioning obedience. The young men of 1895 who left the farms for the cities were undoubtedly more unruly than those who remained docilely on the farms, and the post-war youth who wears a checked shirt and drives a car is less likely to be a filial son then the boy who has spent most of his time poring over account books in his father's shop. We must deplore the excesses of some members of the liberated generation, but at the same time sympathize with, rather than censure, the attempts of others to impart to Japanese culture today some of the personal freedom characteristic of modern culture elsewhere.

The greatest threat to the old order, however, may be something far less dramatic than the burning protests of the young intellectuals. The rapid growth in recent years of a distinctly "middle-brow" culture has gently but insistently shaken the hierarchical organization of Japanese society. The fact that the Emperor listens to the same radio programs as a farmer and wears clothes

34 *It rains a great deal every-where in Japan, but Kanazawa in particular is known as a "town of rain," broad-rimmed rain hats, straw capes, and high rubber boots.*

almost identical to those of a bank teller is in itself startling when one remembers that traditionally the entertainments witnessed by the Emperor were of a sombre, extremely dignified nature, and that an elaborate hierarchy of colors and articles of costume dictated what he wore. Only since the war has the Emperor been permitted to attend Kabuki plays, and now he watches the antics of television performers along with the rest of the country. If he reads a newspaper it will be the same newspaper read by millions of other Japanese, not a special report couched in language suitable for an emperor.

The growth of mass media has affected all classes in Japan from the Emperor downwards. Farmers on an outing are likely to talk about the subjects featured in the popular weekly magazines—the marriage of a certain film star, or the victory of a Japanese car in an international automobile race. Even if these farmers do not consciously wish to upset any traditional ways, the fact that they discuss such matters instead of confining themselves to local gossip, that they wear business suits and neckties and their wives wear nylon stockings, and that they travel frequently to the cities in search of entertainment, means that they know their "place" in society less distinctly than their fathers did.

This is true particularly of the post-war generation. The colorful playboys in their sailboats have captured the imagination of writers about young Japan, but their number is small, and they do not differ essentially from similar groups of rebels and eccentrics of the past fifty years. However, the post-war education and the spread of middle-brow entertainments and literature have affected a very large part of the youth even in the remote countryside, and the changes in the ways of thinking of a whole new generation are more likely to affect the structure of Japanese society than the flamboyant gesture of a few spoiled young men. One critic has put it, "I wonder if the central energy for destroying the old Japanese social customs and for creating new personal and social relationships is not dormant in the 'middle-classed' post-war generation."

The new Japan, the Japan in which democracy and individual liberties are considered the natural right of each individual, is still a long way from materialization. This is not surprising when one considers how short a time it has been since the opening of the country to Western ideas, and how very short a time indeed since defeat in war brought the first real freedom of speech. The old order is still strong, and wherever it is crumbling people are already regretting it. The dream of choosing from the West only what would help preserve the traditional society of Japan proved to be chimerical, and before the kind of society that the young people of Japan now wish for can be brought into being, many more unattractive and even painful changes will assuredly come about. Yet even if an entirely new Japan is born we can be sure that many of the essential traditions will continue to lie under the surface, this time not as the impassive obstacle to progress but as the solid foundation on which Japanese culture must be built.

35 A strange union of the old and the new: a Tokyo drugstore placard in the American style shows a kimono-clad figure offering tranquilizers.

36 Weekly magazines featuring sex, crime and gossip are extremely popular, especially with travelers who have an hour or two to kill.

35

BILL HOMAN

36

37

MARC RIBOUD: MAGNUM

38

MARC RIBOUD: MAGNUM

Chapter IV

A JAPANESE LIFE

CHILDHOOD AND YOUTH

37-38 *Even in a Tokyo street the old etiquette may still persist, but a woman customer in a Tokyo restaurant greets the cook in Western style.*

JAPAN is a wonderful place to be a small child. The birth of every child is celebrated as a welcome event, no matter how numerous a family may already be; a child is a "treasure" in a country where poor people have few others. No sacrifice is too great for parents to make in order to spare their "treasures" any hardships. They are determined that the child's early years shall be happy, and all Japan joins them in this endeavor. Strangers on a crowded streetcar offer children (though not old women) their seats, and the audience at a theater seems completely undisturbed when a baby's howling all but drowns out a performance.

Some outstanding poets and novelists have devoted the major part of their careers to writing for children, with such success that nursery songs are popular even with fully grown adults. The Japanese house itself appears to have been designed to afford a small child the maximum opportunities for mischief: nothing prevents him from penetrating to every corner, and numerous paper *shoji* panels await the smashing of his little fists. The child need not fear harsh words from his mother if he is naughty. He may pummel her mercilessly without exciting more than an indulgent laugh. His grandparents are eager to spoil him with innumerable sweets. He may indeed develop into a little demon without anybody worrying very much; experience has shown that before long the system will bring him into line.

During his first years a child lives almost as a part of his mother's body. Wherever she goes she takes him along, often on her back in a special garment designed for that purpose. If he becomes hungry she immediately suckles him, no matter where they may be. At night he sleeps by her side. A Japanese mother is not concerned about making her son independent of her or, for that matter, about teaching him that he cannot always have his way. Instead, her efforts are focused on prolonging the period of his happy infancy. She encourages him to use a special baby-talk—one popular belief is that infants are incapable of pronouncing the letter "s"—which may be his usual idiom until he begins to attend school.

According to old Japanese customs, probably a result of the high mortality rate among children, a child was considered to "belong to the gods" until he reached the age of seven. If he died before then, he was buried with great simplicity, as though he had never really belonged to his family. Once safely past that age, an occasion marked even now by pilgrimages of children to local shrines, he was ready to begin his new life as a full-fledged child, and he was sent to school with other children. This was a big change for him, and even today a Japanese child's first day at school is a far stranger experience than it is for a Western child. For one thing, he faces in the teacher an authority who will not yield to his caprices, a first indication that his days in paradise are coming to an end. To mark his new status, he must wear a school uniform, a black high-buttoned tunic and short pants. He also learns to call his schoolmates not by their first names as hitherto but by their surnames, with the suffix *kun* (meaning something like "master"). For many children the schoolroom is the first experience of a Western-style building, a place where they must accommodate themselves to tables and chairs instead of familiar *tatami* (mats). This sets off life at school even more markedly from that at home. People begin to expect different things of the child: when he was small they delighted in his high spirits, but good behavior is expected of an elementary school pupil, and a modern teacher who is reluctant to curb a child's exuberance may even be accused of encouraging disrespect towards the child's parents.

At thirteen, about the time when in former days a boy would be inducted into manhood with appropriate ceremony, he enters middle school, an event signalized by his putting on long pants. He ceases to add the honorific *kun* to his friends' names, and he adopts a rough manner of speech. He has by now surrendered most of the privileges of childhood, and the next five or six years are apt to be the most painful of his whole life. This is not so much because (as anywhere in the world) the boy is tormented by the pangs of growing up and adolescent love, as because of his increasing awareness of the demands of the system into which he must fit. He may try to resist by reading Marx and Lenin and other prophets of change, or by abandoning himself to the wilder varieties of American jazz. But no matter what form his attempted escape takes, the fact remains that he is born to a certain position in the Japanese hierarchy, and it will be hard to improve it. Even in Japan, however, there are famous instances of youths who have risen from rags to riches. "Boys, be ambitious!" was the motto which a nineteenth-century American educator tried to

39 *Rush hour on the Tokyo subway.*

40–41 *The lucky ones whisk through the traffic on motorcycles, while others squat and wait for streetcars.*

39

MARC RIBOUD: MAGNUM

40

JAPAN CAMERA INFORMATION CENTER, NEW YORK

41

instill in his Japanese pupils. But the ambitious boys of today generally aspire no higher than becoming white-collar workers—functionaries in business or the government. Most Japanese girls would probably prefer to marry such a man rather than one in business for himself.

FIRST JOB

It is extremely difficult to win a post in the government or in a major firm without a diploma from one of the five or six leading universities. Young men are so desperately anxious to be admitted to these universities that they will take the entrance examinations over and over until they at last pass, rather than admit defeat. They know that once they elect to attend a small university their place is irrevocably determined far down in the hierarchy. A graduate of a lesser university stands no chance of freeing himself from that stigma. If he chooses the academic world as his profession, he can never gain acceptance as a first-rate scholar, regardless of the studies he may subsequently publish. However, even if a young man keeps alight his hopes of rising in the hierarchy by graduating from a leading university, he is by no means assured of the kind of job he wants. There may be several thousand candidates for a single desirable vacancy.

The situation is harder still for the young woman who aspires to a career. Though educational and employment opportunities for her have improved since the war, women university graduates are unlikely to find any suitable place in the business or professional world. Many women and men with only high school educations accept jobs with their families.

A man's first job is not only his most important one, but may be the only one he will ever hold. In many cases he remains with the same company as long as he is able to work. Employees are not often fired, and once a man has been accepted into the "family" of a big company, he cannot easily leave. Not only are the chances of finding another job limited, but the employee quickly establishes many kinds of bonds of obligation and duty. His first job marks so important a milestone in a man's life that it obliges him to change not only his attire but his whole personality. He is no longer a student in uniform, but must look the part of a "salaryman" in a dark-blue suit with a briefcase under his arm. He now reads popular, middle-brow magazines instead of the intellectual journals he favored in college days, and he is expected to speak with pride of the traditions of his company, although only a year or two before he may have been attacking it as a vicious agency of monopolistic capitalism. He will probably be sincere in this change of heart. He now calls his associates *san* (Mr.) and is careful to observe the proprieties of honorifics with them.

Life in a large Japanese office is not very pleasant for the junior executive.

42   The kimono was not designed for the hurly-burly of trolley cars, but many Japanese women continue to prefer these traditional garments.

He will find that not only is it organized into a rigid hierarchy, but it is often split into rival cliques. Different factions are constantly jockeying for power, watching with suspicion the activities of "enemy" groups. An innocent lunch appointment may be interpreted as a "gathering of forces"; a casual remark may be lent sinister implications in the hope of discrediting a rival. But the young man cannot easily avoid entanglement in such divisions. The way up the ladder in a big company is slow, and may depend more than anything on success in such machinations.

MARRIAGE

Once the young man is comfortably settled in a job his parents are likely to begin asking people to help find a suitable wife for him. A go-between is indispensable, and people are normally delighted to accept this task. In some parts of the country it is said that a man who has not arranged at least three marriages is a failure as a human being, and perhaps even city-dwellers feel something of this responsibility. (In some cases, however, the go-between seems to be moved also by the anticipation of gifts from the couple he unites.) The young man may inform the go-between of his preference in girls—whether he likes them with round or long faces, a matter of great importance to Japanese men—but normally he leaves the arrangement of the marriage to the discretion of his parents. Despite all the romantic literature produced in Japan during the past half-century, marriage is considered to be essentially a union between families, particularly by people of the middle and upper classes. Love suicides by young couples whose parents have refused them permission to marry still figure prominently in the newspapers, but they represent not a revolt against the prevailing system so much as a tacit recognition of its authority. Love marriages, though much discussed, are relatively uncommon.

When the go-between has discovered a likely spouse for the young man, the two families exchange documents and carefully weigh the relative advantages of a union. Nothing is overlooked: the remote ancestry of both parties is scrutinized for traces of disqualifying illnesses, and property, education and social connections are carefully checked. Astrological factors sometimes can have an overriding importance. A girl born in the Year of the Horse may be rejected for no other reason, or an otherwise eminently suitable match be rendered undesirable by the single fact that the boy and girl are separated by a difference of four years in age—four being an unlucky number. Because go-betweens are notoriously given to exaggerating the merits of their candidates, indirect inquiries are also made to determine whether or not the girl is thrifty, hard-working and possesses the other virtues. If, after the examination is completed, the verdict is favorable, the go-between arranges a meeting of

43 *Spring in Japan: cherry blossoms, and the uncertain glory of April sunshine. Saké is sold in booths along the paths, but many people bring their own.*

44 Maiko *dancers (apprentice geishas) pause by the "Weeping Cherry Blossoms" of the Heian Shrine in Kyoto.*

43

44

the prospective couple. Usually either of the young people has the privilege of rejecting the other, but acceptance of the parents' wishes is more common.

If all has gone smoothly, a "lucky day" is chosen for the wedding. Certain days must be avoided. The Day of the Monkey (*saru*) is taboo because another word meaning "to leave" has the same pronounciation, and a girl who marries on a *saru* day may therefore leave her husband. The Day of the Tiger is shunned because of a saying that a tiger may travel a thousand miles, but it always returns, suggesting that a bride will return divorced to her old home. April is not a popular month for marriages because the cherry blossoms scatter then; a wedding gift with a design of maple-leaves is also considered unlucky because leaves scatter sooner or later. Modern families may not actually believe in the magic of word associations, but they nevertheless tend to follow the old traditions in choosing a day for the ceremony.

The wedding is considered the most important event in the lives of the couple, and as such is the occasion for extravagant spending, even by those who can ill afford it. A proper bridal costume has sleeves which trail almost to the floor and the obi requires as much material as a whole kimono. It costs hundreds of dollars and may never be worn again, for the changes in bridal kimono styles are rapid and pronounced. It is possible nowadays to hire a kimono for the wedding, but the Japanese fondness for extravagance persists. The ceremony also involves the expense of a great spread of delicacies which must, according to tradition, come from both the mountains and the sea. The parents of the bride are determined to provide fitting entertainments for the guests, knowing that tongues will wag at any signs of economy.

Most weddings take place "before the Shinto gods." This may simply mean that a scroll with the name of a god hangs in the *tokonoma* before which the couple exchange vows, but usually a Shinto priest will preside, exorcising any evil influences which may be present with a shake of the streamers of his wand. The most important moment in the ceremony is the ritual drinking of saké by the couple—three times, three times again, and finally nine times in all. No words need be said, and there is no ring or other emblem of the marriage, but after drinking the saké the bride removes her hat of white floss silk, signifying that she has left her old family. It is said that the practice of wearing this hat originated in the custom of the groom not seeing his bride's face until after the ceremony was completed; it was feared that if he saw it before he might not wish to go through with the wedding.

Some modern weddings are performed "before the meal," in both senses of the expression—in the banqueting hall of a department store where the eating, drinking and merrymaking of the feast immediately follow the ceremony. At formal receptions the newlyweds sit at the head of a long table; the bride's and groom's families are seated on opposite sides. The sponsor of the marriage—sometimes the original go-between, but often the head of the

45   Japanese visit their cemeteries frequently and view them without fear; this one serves as a park in crowded Tokyo.

groom's firm or his senior professor or a superior civil servant—sits with the newlyweds, and at a given point in the festivities presents them to the party. He describes their lineages: if no ancestor in the recent past has been especially distinguished, it is always possible to claim that either bride or groom is descended from a tenth-century emperor. The attainments of each are lovingly recounted: the groom has always been unusual in his diligence and modesty, the bride is proficient at flower arrangement and at playing the piano.

These formalities are followed by the various guests singing auspicious passages from the Nô plays as well as ditties of a less elevated nature. One part of the festivities, in some country districts at least, involves a token beating of the bride or groom. There are also survivals of an old custom of bodily placing the newlyweds in bed. On the night of the wedding the young men of the village are apt to break holes into the *shoji* to peep at the couple and to make raucous comments. The modern couple is likely to avoid such indignities by leaving at once on a honeymoon to such favorite spots as the hot springs at Atami or the mountains at Hakone.

The young man, who has been timid and polite to his bride up until the marriage, now adopts the abrupt tones expected of him as a husband. No matter how affectionate he may feel, he does not wish to expose himself to ridicule by seeming to dote on his wife or to stand in awe of her. The wife, on the other hand, must always employ a full range of honorifics in addressing her husband. She will never call him by his first name, nor will she ever dare, in public at least, to suggest that she has claims to his attention. If they go on a honeymoon this may well be the only journey of their lives together. Indeed, it would not be unusual if from that time on they never went together to a film, a restaurant or even for a walk. If they have a house of their own, the wife is generally left behind to watch over it—Japanese houses cannot be left unattended—while the husband is away; if they live in his parents' house, the bride's mother-in-law sees to it that she enjoys few moments of leisure.

FIRST CHILD

The next important event in their lives is the birth of their first child. Japanese generally hope that the first child will be a girl and the second a boy, the supposition being that a girl will help take care of her baby brother. Each step in the infant's life is marked by traditional rituals. Parents, particularly in the country, are careful to observe them all scrupulously in order that the child may grow up healthy and prosperous. On the third day after the baby's birth, for example, he wears his first garment with sleeves. On the seventh day he is given his name—sometimes simply a number like "first," but often a name derived from those of his parents or grandparents. Its meaning is important. For example, if the surname is "Pond Field" (*Ikeda*) a boy may be given the personal name of "Pure" (*Kiyoshi*) because it is, of course, desirable that the waters of a pond be pure. Attention is also paid to the total number of strokes needed to write the characters for the child's names; it is believed that an unlucky number may permanently blight his future.

About a month after the baby is born he is taken for the first time to the neighborhood Shinto shrine to be presented to the god of the shrine as one of his "children." Baby's first outing must conform to the customs of his part of the country. In central Japan, for example, the parents give sweets to all children encountered on baby's journey to the shrine; money is scattered every time a bridge is crossed; and the shrine itself must be approached without passing under a *torii* gate. In some villages the parents deliberately make the baby cry when he reaches the shrine in order that the god may hear him and recognize his new "child." In other places the baby is encouraged to make water in front of the *torii* of the shrine as a first step in toilet training. On the hundredth day the child is fed his first rice, marking his initiation into the community.

PLEASURES OF ORDINARY LIFE

The father fulfills one of the sacred requirements of filial piety by begetting heirs for the family, and he has the further responsibility of providing for their support. However, he is not expected to show much affection to his children. He may be too exhausted by the strains of work at the office to pay them much attention, or he may find home such a dull place that he will tend increasingly to spend his evenings drinking with friends rather than playing with his children. Even if he stays at home in the evenings, he is likely to be absorbed by some pastime of his own which may become the dominant interest of his life. Recent Japanese novelists have devoted many pages to describing the tensions in the life of office workers; the monotony and thanklessness of the work they perform; and the tedium of their life at home. These books have the ring of authenticity, though they do not often make enjoyable reading. They are incomplete, moreover, in at least one feature: they tend to omit all mention of the aesthetic pleasures which relieve the boredom of the lives of many businessmen and functionaries.

Innumerable arts and hobbies can be counted as popular distractions, including flower-arranging, calligraphy, music, the growing of plants, and the collection of books or objects of art. Such pursuits are not, as in most countries, the recreation of a handful of wealthy and cultivated amateurs. There are, for example, about fifty monthly magazines with a total circulation of over a million copies which are devoted entirely to poetry. Most of the readers are ordinary office and factory employees and not professional literary people. One may suddenly hear the strains of a Nô play coming from the back of a small stationery shop, where the owner is practicing, and a brusque newspaper reporter may display an unexpected talent for the classical Japanese dance. A housewife whose children are grown and no longer need her constant attention may devote her new leisure to learning to play the samisen or to batik dyeing. In any random selection of Japanese businessmen one is likely to find almost every art represented.

Another pleasure shared by all Japanese, no matter how dreary their lives may seem to the novelists, is the delight in the changes brought by the seasons. This goes back very far with the Japanese. In the year 1212 Kamo no Chomei, a monk who had abandoned human society to live in a lonely retreat, expressed his abiding attachment for at least one pleasure of the world: "My only desire for this life is to see the beauties of the changing seasons." One probable reason why the Japanese have always placed such importance on the seasons—it is required in the composition of *haiku,* for example, that the season be unmistakeably indicated—is that the four seasons are so clearly and agreeably defined in Japan. Moreover, despite frequent moans over the winter cold or the summer heat, the Japanese enjoy experiencing these appropriate attributes of the seasons. The Tokyo house, unlike the New York apartment, affords very little protection against the rigors of the weather, and the first warm day of spring after a hard winter consequently brings genuine pleasure. The Japanese not only recognize but respond to the seasons: formerly, days were fixed when winter garments were changed for summer ones, and regardless of whether the "clothes-changing" day happened to be hot or cold, people obeyed. Even today many Japanese regularly start wearing long underwear from the first of October, or change to straw hats on the first of July.

Each season has its special food. A steaming bowl of noodles is a real delight in a Japanese house heated only by a couple of lumps of charcoal, and the first bamboo shoots or the first eggplants taste better if one has waited for them than if they are available throughout the year in frozen packets. When one goes to an elegant Japanese restaurant one usually does not specify what one wishes to eat. It is customary instead to let the cooks decide which fish, vegetables and fruit are at their best that day. Freshness and appropriateness to the season are prized more highly than the actual preparation; the most important thing in Japanese cuisine is that each dish retain its natural flavor and that it be served at the moment of greatest perfection. The favorite food of most Japanese is raw fish—not any raw fish, but the variety which tastes best at a particular season or place. It is not surprising therefore that many foreigners find Japanese cooking excessively bland and uninteresting. To a Japanese, on the other hand, European cuisines seem uniform in their disregard of seasons.

The changing beauties of nature are a source of joy for Japanese businessmen

46 Springtime streets are bright with flowers that were never alive and will never wither unless the dyes run off.

47

48

and workers no less than they were for hermits of the past. In spring the parks famous for their cherry blossoms are crowded with visitors from all walks of life. The steel mills charter special busses to carry the workers to temples outside Kyoto, and distant mountainsides attract farmers and fishermen. Special excursions in summer take city-dwellers to watch the fireflies or to enjoy the cool of evening by some river bank. The September moon, the "famous moon" of Japanese poetry, is now viewed by thousands at the sites loved by the old poets, such as the pond where the poet Bashô once spent the evening walking round and round, admiring the reflected moon. In autumn the changing colors of the leaves draw millions, and the hardest-headed businessman will not begrudge a day spent viewing the maples. In winter, of course, there are snowy landscapes; the garden of the Silver Pavilion in Kyoto or the brilliantly colored carving of the architecture at Nikko take on new beauties in the snow.

Not everyone can afford to travel to Nikko for snow-viewing or to Takao for the maple leaves, but thanks to the bargain rates offered by the railways and bus companies, such excursions form part of the new middle-class culture, and are by no means the privilege of the rich. Even if a trip to see the cherry blossoms at some celebrated spot entails financial hardships a needy family is likely to go anyway.

Japanese frugality is traditionally balanced by a love of extravagance. The Kyoto man, otherwise so parsimonious, will wear luxurious clothes, and the calculating Osaka businessman is apt to be an epicure. Such extravagances are not frowned on because of the old habit of considering the year to be divided into ordinary (*ke*) and special (*hare*) days. Most of these "special" days, even those now observed in the most secular manner, originally had religious significance. Because they tended to coincide with the blossoming of the peach trees or some other pleasant event in nature, they afforded the Japanese the occasion to break the monotony of their ordinary lives with cheerful and even reckless merrymaking. For centuries the rulers of Japan tried to curb this inclination towards extravagance among the commoners, but always without success. What developed instead was an ability to conceal one's indulgence in luxury behind a facade of austere simplicity. The plain black outer coat (*haori*) of a Japanese gentleman may be lined with brocade worked in gold thread, and a woman's under kimono, all but invisible save at the neck line, may be a miracle of dyeing. Again, the hut where the tea ceremony is performed may seem at first glance to be the simplest possible structure, devoid of any suggestion of pretense or luxury. Yet such a hut usually costs more to build than a mansion, for every detail is exquisitely finished. The vertical beam by the *tokonoma,* for example, may appear to be just another twisted tree trunk, but connoisseurs will recognize it as a wood of the greatest rarity. The implements used in the tea ceremony are also deceptively unassuming: a bamboo whisk

47   *Shoes must be removed at the door of every Japanese-style building, no matter how up-to-date it is. Slippers are usually supplied.*

48   *Tokyo has beer gardens in cellars and on roof tops. The decor varies from old Bavarian to severe modern, and the Japanese beer is excellent.*

one might buy for a few cents, a rusty old kettle, some cups of unfinished pottery, a little canister for the tea. Each one of these, however, may be worth a fortune if it has the right pedigree.

Whatever form it may take, the importance of extravagance is almost universally recognized. Nobody praises the prudent parents who economize with their daughther's wedding, nor the children wo are thrifty when arranging their parents' funeral. Nor does a guest appreciate it if, when he comes to dinner, he is treated as "one of the family" and given ordinary fare. The difference between "special" and "ordinary" is probably nowhere more conspicuous than in Japan, and the promise of some future "special" dinner is what keeps people going through innumerable insipid meals of "ordinary" food. Sometimes frugality and extravagance go hand in hand. In a city like Tokyo office workers generally buy a bowl of noodles at fifty yen for their lunch, and then go next door for a cup of coffee at sixty yen. The noodles contain the nutrition, but the luxury of coffee gives them their savor.

Extravagance, at whatever level he can manage, makes the life of a Japanese more cheerful than tables of per caput income might show. A Japanese whose income is the same as a European worker's will live much more poorly during most days of the month, eating a monotonous diet and wearing the same clothes every day, but once or twice, or more often if he can, he enjoys the pleasures of luxury, spending money which a European worker would prefer to distribute over the whole month. At the other end of the scale, a rich Japanese usually lives in a house which is very modest by Western standards, but if he goes to a restaurant or geisha house, it represents an extravagance few Westerners are willing to undertake. In either case the Japanese is content with less on ordinary days for the pleasure of the "special" days of celebration.

49 Most Japanese, even in the big cities, dislike the idea of living in apartments, but a few handsome new buildings have been erected in Tokyo.

OLD AGE

The partiality for luxuries often grows stronger with age. The Japanese who retires after long years of catering to the wishes of his superiors can look forward to an old age in which his own whims will be humored and his cravings for little extravagances indulged. He may collect pottery or stones, or raise chrysanthemums. If he is lucky he will live in Kyoto, a city full of amenities for the aged—temples to visit, sermons for their benefit, tea ceremonies and traditional entertainments. One can often see old people trouping through the precincts of a shrine, led by a leader with a flag while they themselves are identified by strips of magenta or green ribbon pinned to their coats. They clutch albums in which to affix the stamp of the temple or shrine, proving they have really made the visit. The riches of the Japanese past, often ignored during youth and middle age, become a great source of joy to those in retirement.

YASUO TOMISHIGE: JAPAN CAMERA INFORMATION CENTER

MARC RIBOUD: MAGNUM

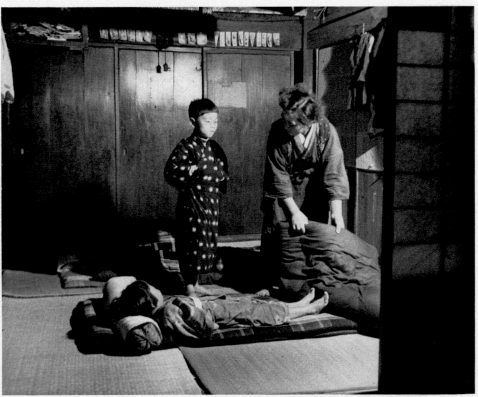

ORLANDO: THREE LIONS

The more scholarly may choose to devote their remaining years to the study of the biography of some ancient poet. The fact that a man may have had little schooling and spent his whole life in running a shop is no obstacle if he wishes to undertake such a study, and his diligent perusal of musty records may eventually uncover new information—the profession of his chosen poet's uncle, or the name of the illness from which the poet's third daughter died.

The old man or old woman enjoys greater freedom of speech than anyone in Japan. He may omit honorifics without worrying himself or others; he may relate his opinions, however bizarre, without bothering to estimate the possible effect on the hearers; and he may be as bawdy as he pleases. He may wear Japanese or Western dress or an outlandish combination of both without exciting comment. He may indulge himself in liquor and rich foods or be content with a Spartan diet. Public meeting of Communists and right-wing fanatics alike are filled with old people; younger men often hesitate to be seen at such gatherings, but an old man has nothing to lose. If he lives to be eighty or ninety, he will be venerated as a sage, and his most trivial utterance will be accorded respectful attention.

DEATH

No matter how indifferent to religious matters a man may have been during his lifetime, when he dies he is virtually certain to be buried in accordance with Buddhist rites. This is a legacy of the Tokugawa Period when, as one method of controlling the menace of Christianity, all Japanese were required to affiliate themselves with a Buddhist temple. When an atheist dies today, his burial is likely to be considered a family affair and not a private matter, and for the family's reputation a priest will be summoned.

The dead man's body is placed with the head to the north (following the example of Buddha who, it is said, died in that position) in front of the Buddhist altar in his house. Word is sent out of his death, and relatives and friends assemble at the house to mourn him. A Buddhist priest prays by his pillow. The corpse is washed and dressed in a white garment—as in China, white is the color of mourning. Later it is placed in a coffin together with a few objects (such as a favorite tea cup or a pipe). Copper coins are also placed in the coffin in some parts of Japan, to pay the boatman's fee across Sanzu River, the River Styx of the Japanese afterworld, or to enable the dead man's ghost to buy himself some sweets when he comes back as a ghost to haunt this world. Interment is still commonly practiced in country districts, but in the cities cremation is now the rule. The funeral service follows the burial. Commemorative observances are held at weekly intervals until the 49th day after the death, and after that there are less frequent memorial prayers—on the

50   Clad in kimonos and seated on traditional tatami mats, a family watches television.

51   Any room may serve as sleeping quarters in a Japanese house. A mattress spread on the tatami, quilts laid over it, a pillow – and the bed is made.

first, third, seventh, thirteenth years and some later anniversaries. Gradually, however, the memory of the individual who died fades, and respect is paid to him as one of many ancestors. His own grave loses its importance, and his descendants pay their homage instead to a symbolic tomb which honors all the ancestors. Unless a man has unusual achievements to his credit, it does not take long for him to become only a name in the family records, despite the worship paid him.

PRIVATE AND PUBLIC LIFE

A Japanese comes closest to the ways of his ancestors at the beginning and end of his life. During his lifetime he is constantly being confronted by situations unknown a hundred years ago. Perhaps the most striking difference between old and new is the importance which public life has assumed today, though it was almost insignificant in the past. Women of respectable families, for example, seldom left their immediate neighborhoods, and men normally frequented only well-established routes, like those leading to the gay quarters. There were no parks, squares, cafés, meeting halls or salons, and the arts appropriate to such places—oratory, drawing-room comedy and the rest—were unknown. The only place where large numbers of people gathered regularly was the theater, a necessity imposed by the impossibility of giving separate performances for each party. Most entertainments, however, were held in private rooms. As has been suggested, the "vertical" relationships between lord and vassal, father and child, elder brother and younger brother, were carefully plotted, and the last detail of what constituted the proper conduct for each of these parties was common knowledge. The philosophers rarely, however, discussed how a man should behave towards strangers—one of the most important parts of the Western code of manners.

Even today, strangers simply do not exist for most Japanese. If one steps on a stranger's foot there is no need to say "Excuse me" or even acknowledge by a gesture that something has happened. One is obliged, on the other hand, to apologize almost automatically to every acquaintance who comes within speaking distance, "The other day I was very rude." Until very recently one was expected when passing acquaintances in the street to draw in one's breath as a mark of respect; but it was permissible before strangers on a train to sneeze, yawn, belch or pick one's teeth without bothering to cover one's mouth. In the West we tend to be more concerned about strangers than about family or friends: it is all right to pick up a bone at table in one's house but not in a restaurant; one may lounge about the house in scanty attire if it is hot, though one would not dream of stripping in public; and even if a man's desk at home is a mess, he tries to keep his office looking neat and efficient. In Japan the practice is precisely the opposite. Anything goes providing it is in front of strangers. In a restaurant one may slurp one's soup with gusto, though at home respect for a stern parent may impose silence. The Japanese gentleman thinks nothing of stripping to his underwear before strangers on a train, but if relaxing in the comfort of his home, will hastily dress at word that an acquaintance is coming. The Japanese house is a model of neatness, but a Japanese office is likely to be in chaotic disorder.

The contrasts between private and public behavior take even more striking forms. The same man who is exquisitely courteous to his acquaintances will savagely rip his way through a crowd in order to be sure of getting a seat on a train, even when it is unlikely he will have to stand. The man who loves the quiet beauty of a suburban street, where every footfall sounds clearly and the chirps of insects tell the season, will furiously honk the horn of his automobile when driving along the same street. Anyone who has ever seen the incredible litter left under the cherry blossoms knows how indifferent the Japanese are to the effect that their leavings may have on the sensibilities of those who come after them to view the blossoms.

Complaints about Japanese behavior in public may be found very early. In the year 1330, for example, the monk Kenkô described the antics of ill-bred people:

"They squirm and struggle to get under the blossoms, they stare intently, they drink wine, they link verses, and at last they heartlessly break off great branches. They dip their hands and feet in springs; they get down and step on the snow, leaving footmarks; there is nothing they do not regard as their own." But it has only been in the past half-century or so, with the introduction of the Western variety of public life, that it has become a matter of everyday concern. The Japanese authorities in the 80's and 90's, anxious lest the foreigners find their ways contemptible or uncivilized, ordered rickshaw pullers and other laborers to wear more than the traditional loincloth, and prohibited mixed bathing. Such conspicuous conflicts with the European sense of decency and morality could be modified by decrees, but respect for the feelings of unknown strangers was not easily nurtured in a society organized on hierarchical lines. The "horizontal" relations of Japanese could not be altered by edict to coincide with those of peoples accustomed for many centuries to public life.

Of late one may detect a gradual change, however, emanating from the main cities. The trains traveling between Tokyo and Osaka are less likely to be left ankle-deep in litter after a night's journey than those in outlying districts. The indifference towards public buildings, and indeed towards all buildings where one is not required to remove one's shoes before entering, also seems to be giving way to more Western ideas of maintenance and public responsibility. If such changes gain wider currency they are bound to effect not only public but private life, for the two are inevitably connected.

Chapter V

FOUR FAITHS

AMONG the most powerful impressions a visitor takes from Japan are those connected with the Japanese religions. The pagoda wrapped in Kyoto mists on a winter's day, the great *torii* rising out of the Inland Sea, the ruined church which stands as a memento of the atomic bomb dropped on Nagasaki—all are sights which can never be forgotten. Almost every village, however unimportant, is dominated by the massive tiled roof of its Buddhist temple, and its spot of greatest scenic beauty is likely to be occupied by a Shinto shrine.

The visitor may be forgiven if initially he has trouble telling a Buddhist temple from a Shinto shrine, and if the distinctions among the many sects of Buddhism escape him. Yet he will notice some differences. For example, Shinto shrines are usually simple structures devoid of images, while the more imposing Buddhist temples are likely to be filled with a rich collection of statues and paintings. The Shinto priests wear robes of pastel shades, while the Buddhist priests are clothed in black.

If the visitor, intrigued by these differences, asks how many Japanese are Shintoists and how many Buddhists, he will be informed that almost every Japanese is both. If he then asks whom the Japanese worship as the supreme being, he may be given a bewildering variety of answers. Religion is a complicated matter in Japan, more so perhaps than in most countries. At least four faiths affect the lives of the Japanese.

Shinto, the native religion, means literally "the way of the gods." Eight million or more gods have been worshipped, including birds, beasts, trees, plants, mountains, and even evil demons. Shinto activity is centered around shrines, but in every house there is also a "god-shelf" where offerings are made, especially at New Year. Shinto has no ethical teachings of its own which Japanese are expected to obey. Its sacred book, *The Record of Ancient Matters*

52 In a Shinto temple, a priest announces the ceremony by blowing on a conch shell.

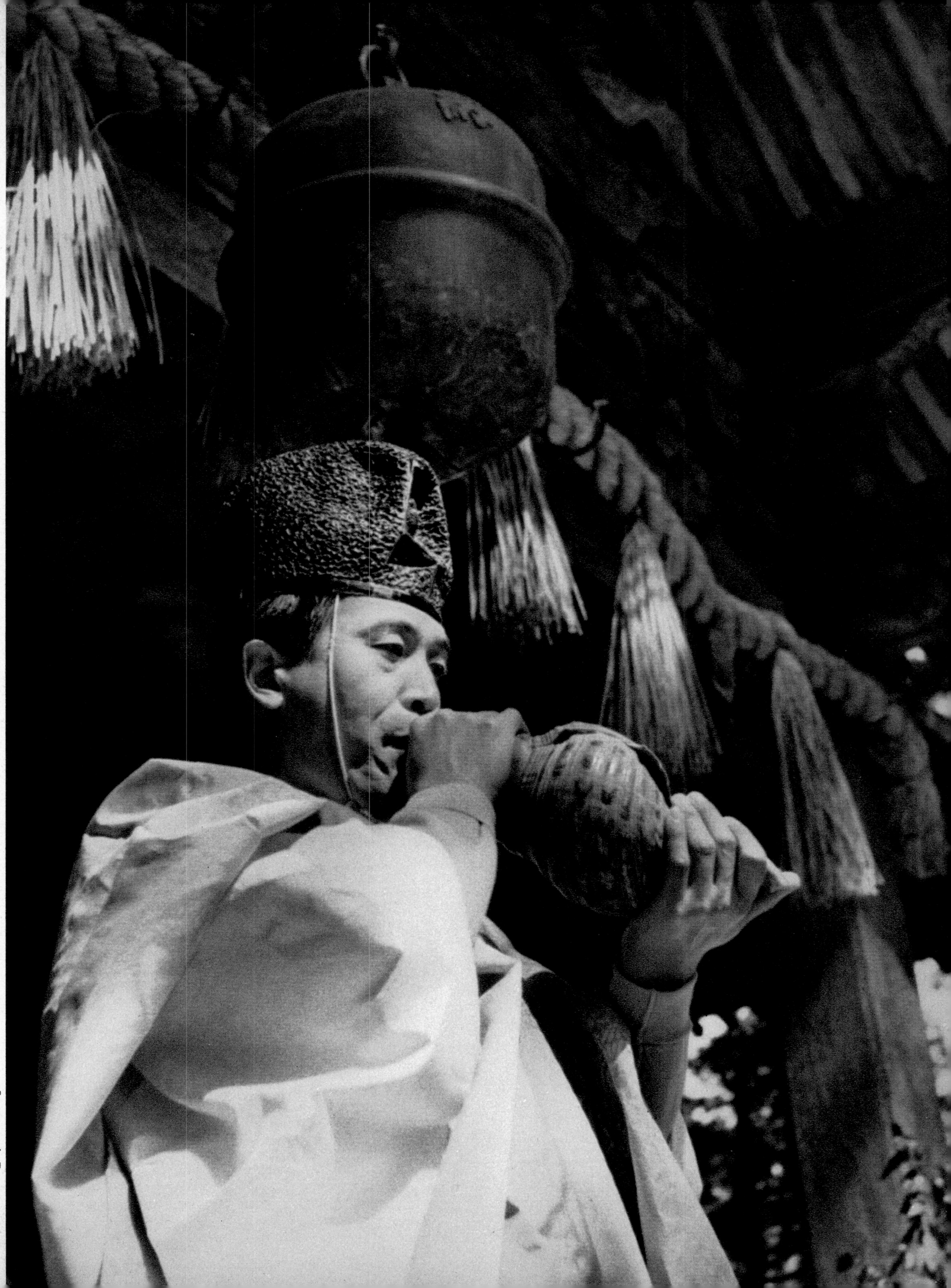

Sheldon A. Brody

53   WERNER BISCHOF: MAGNUM

54   SANFORD H. ROTH: RAPHO GUILLUMETTE

(*Kojiki*), consists not of religious admonitions but of legends about the gods and their descendants, the emperors.

In contrast to Shinto, which began as an inarticulate collection of rites derived from the worship of nature, ancestors and heroes, Buddhism was a highly developed religion by the time it was introduced to Japan in the sixth century A.D. Its beginnings are traced back to the historical Buddha, a man who was born in northern India in the sixth century B.C. and preached his religion widely. An enormous body of theological writings was produced by Indian and Chinese scholars before Buddhism reached Japan, and there were many schools differing from one another at least as much as the different branches of Christianity do. In Japan a half dozen sects must be distinguished.

Confucianism, another of the Japanese faiths, is the name given to the teachings of Confucius, the Chinese sage who lived 551 to 479 B.C. Though Confucianism is not, strictly speaking, a religion, and says nothing about an afterworld, at times the veneration paid to Confucius has differed little from that accorded a god. Confucianism provides the ethical basis of Japanese life.

Christianity was first introduced to Japan in the sixteenth century. After suffering long years of persecution, it emerged in the nineteenth century as one of the important religions. There are several hundred thousand Christians in Japan today.

Each of these four faiths has left its mark on Japanese society, and anyone who desires to go beneath the surface of Japan today must give some time to the often perplexing questions of religion.

53 Shinto priests file into a shrine. They wear the robes and hats of a thousand years ago, and carry tablets which in ancient times were the mark of officials.

SHINTO

The most joyous time of year in any town or village is the annual festival of its Shinto shrine. This is the day, established in remote antiquity, when the enshrined deity descends from heaven to his residence on earth, a day marked by a few solemnities and much general rejoicing. The precincts of the shrine, normally deserted, become the scene of music and dance, of the bustle of priests and assistants in flowing robes, and of wild activity in the merchants' booths ranged along the approaches to the shrine. Most striking of all is the swirling crowd, the whole population of the town, it would seem, swarming through the alleys made by the booths, ringing the bell before the shrine and clapping their hands in worship, buying good-luck charms and soothsayers' predictions, dropping coins in contribution boxes and pinball machines, drinking saké under some trees and relieving themselves under others—in sum, making the most of the god's visitation.

Such a festival is in some ways surprisingly close to the manner of worship of ancient Japan. The religion of the ancients, as we can gather from customs

54 Every year, hundreds of thousands of Japanese visit the immense Todaiji Temple at Nara, originally built in the eighth century.

surviving in some regions today, was communal. Daily prayers by individuals were almost unknown. The whole village would prepare for its annual festival by eating "pure" foods, by ritual ablutions, and in some cases by observing absolute silence for weeks. A tall tree was often erected in the shrine grounds as a kind of stepping-stone for the god on his descent to earth. If the chosen tree was a living one, it was tied with a sacred rope to keep off evil influences. Festivals were always held at night, so that when the god walked abroad no mortal eyes would see him. Even an inadvertent glimpse of the deity might cause death.

One indispensable feature of every festival was a procession, in which the entire population of the village, hierarchically arranged, accompanied the god in his tour of the shrine or escorted him to his "traveling place." Festivals were marked also by a communal meal: the god of the shrine and the worshippers joined in partaking of the same food and liquor—ritually pure offerings prepared over a sacred fire. After the feasting often came orgies induced by the saké and the night.

The main features of Shinto worship have been preserved through the ages, though in details they often differ from ancient practices. The basic acts of worship are still "attendance" and "offering." Today "attendance" usually means merely going to the shrine to pray, though formerly it implied taking an active part in the rituals, including the sacred dances and processions. The chief celebrations, then as now, were those in spring to pray for good weather for the crops, and those in autumn to give thanks for the harvest. One feature of all observances was the insistence on cleanliness and the fear of contamination. Even today worshippers are expected to wash their hands and rinse their mouths before approaching the god. Water has always been considered the source of purity.

Some of the shrines, particularly the chief one at Ise, retain their ancient appearance. Even those whose architecture has been most influenced by Chinese or Buddhist design still have at least a *torii,* the most typical feature of a Shinto shrine. When one attends a ceremony at which priests read prayers written in the sonorous ancient tongue, and girls dressed in crimson and white solemnly dance to hauntingly remote music of a thousand years ago, one may easily be convinced that little has changed in Shinto.

Yet had it not been for the influence of more complex religions and systems of thought—the different varieties of Buddhism, Confucianism, and even Christianity—Shinto might have remained a shamanistic cult similar to those found today on the Asiatic mainland. Shinto was indeed forced to occupy a role of subservience to Buddhism for many centuries, and though it always held the allegiance of the humble folk, it attracted little interest among the aristocrats and intellectuals. Some Japanese theologians, unable to dismiss the native religion altogether, yet convinced of the superiority of Buddhism,

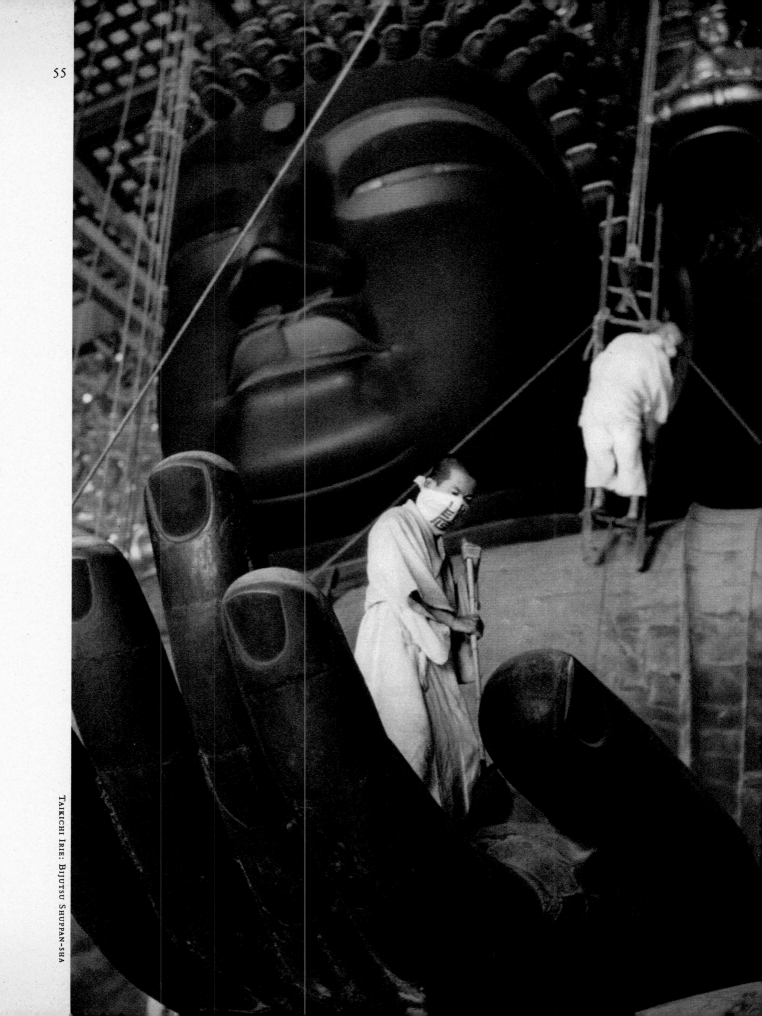

55

TAIKICHI IRIE: BIJUTSU SHUPPAN-SHA

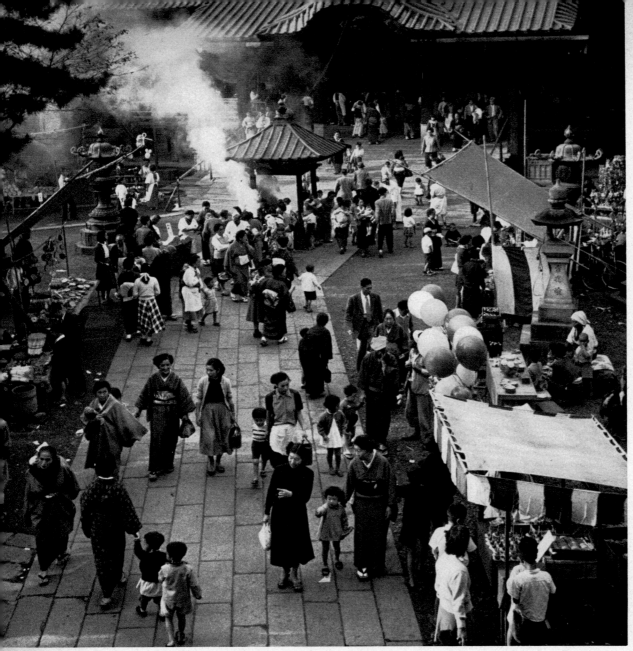

56   HORACE BRISTOL

57

SHELDON A. BRODY

argued that the Shinto gods were actually Buddhist deities who had chosen to manifest themselves in Japan. It became customary for Buddhist temples and Shinto shrines to share the same precincts, because it was believed that the Shinto gods would protect Buddha from native Japanese devils.

The union between Buddhism and Shinto was the most prominent feature of Japanese religious life until the government ordered the religions to separate in 1868. Even today most Japanese are at least nominally Shintoist and Buddhist at the same time. A "shelf" for the gods and an altar for Buddha are found in almost all houses, with each receiving attention and offerings at appropriate times. An outsider might find it hard to see how anyone seriously convinced of either religion could accept the other, for the two are incompatible. The union was made possible only because men can divide their minds and accept contrary things at the same time. As a Shintoist a man believes that the present world is the only desirable one and the afterworld a place of foulness and evil; as a Buddhist he believes that the present world is a place of foulness and evil, and the world to come the only one which offers a chance of happiness. Again, as a Shintoist he believes that the gods procreated the Japanese islands and formed other islands from coagulations in the foam of the sea-water. As a Buddhist, on the other hand, he believes in the eternity of the universe and the absence of a creator. Few men, however, have tried to confront the beliefs. Instead, every possibility of union has been explored with such success that, at the time of the separation, it was not uncommon for a man to be a Shinto and a Buddhist priest at the same time. Christianity also exercised influence on Shinto early in the nineteenth century, by suggesting to Shinto theologians the importance of a single Creator God, supreme among the deities, though Shinto had always been polytheistic.

The closest connection existed between Shinto and the Imperial Family. The Emperor, according to Shinto theology, is the descendant of the Sun Goddess, and his right to rule Japan is based on her divine command. A famous four-teenth-century historical work began with the words, "Japan is the divine country. The Heavenly Ancestor first laid its foundations, and the Sun Goddess left her descendants to reign over it forever and ever. This is true only of our country, and nothing similar may be found in foreign lands. That is why it is called the divine country." Shinto lent itself very readily to nationalism, and developed from a community religion to a national faith which had as its central article of belief the divinity of the Emperor. Its adherents believed that Japan was superior to all other countries because of its unbroken line of rulers.

When the Imperial Family regained power in 1868, one of the first acts of the new regime was to give Shinto the dignity of a state religion. Buddhist temples were stripped of their privileges and even destroyed, while Shinto benefited by the erection of many impressive shrines. The Emperor's role as the chief priest of Shinto was emphasized, and the Shinto gods were carried

56–57 Worshippers leaving a Nichiren Buddhist temple in Tokyo pass stalls where fortunes, souvenirs, and pets are sold.

to the various territories captured by Japanese troops overseas. During the war, students (and sometimes whole towns) were marched off to Shinto shrines to worship *en masse,* and anyone passing a shrine was compelled to bow. Belief in Shinto became a patriotic rather than a religious duty, and few people dared to object. On the other hand, with the defeat of Japan in 1945 and the consequent loss of prestige for the Imperial Family, Shinto suffered an eclipse, and the denationalization of the shrines for a time threatened their survival. Today the major Shinto shrines have regained their prosperity, but smaller ones come to life only for their festivals.

The most important Shinto sanctuary is the Grand Shrine of Ise, situated in the east of Japan at a site of such marvelous scenic beauty as to inspire faith in the gods even among hardened unbelievers. One sees first of all the River Isuzu, limpidly clear even after a storm, where pilgrims perform the ritual ablutions before approaching the shrine. The way to the shrine itself leads through a magnificent avenue of cedars which suggest in their straightness and simple grandeur ideals close to the Japanese. The buildings are not themselves old, but they preserve unchanged the ancient traditions, for, when buildings are erected every twenty years to replace the old ones, they are exact replicas.

In 1953 the fifty-ninth renewal ceremony of the Ise shrine took place. It was unusual in that the expenses of erecting the new shrines were met by popular subscription instead of by state grant, and the invited guests at the ceremony included not only dignitaries of the ecclesiastical and political worlds but farmers and housewives.

Everyone had to be present by three in the afternoon, though the ceremony, in the tradition of the ancient Shinto rites, did not begin until nightfall. The worshippers sat for five or six hours on thin matting spread out on the ground, a feat of physical endurance, but hardly a word was spoken. The towering trees seemed to impose silence, and the faint sounds of traffic and of distant radios in the town seemed to belong to another existence. At dusk lanterns were lighted—at every Japanese festival lanterns are indispensable—and the first procession, emerging from the old shrine, began slowly moving to the new one. These were the carpenters, the thatchers, and all the other workmen who had actually constructed the new shrine. They went by solemnly in their stiff blue robes, proud of their part in the ceremony.

Other processions followed: the high priests of all the great shrines of the land, each bearing one ritual implement; the special envoy of the Emperor (his brother, somewhat disappointingly attired in a frock coat and a silk hat); and finally, in total darkness, the Sun Goddess herself was escorted to her new shrine, in a tent of white silk borne by the priests. In the dead silence the rustle of the priests' robes and the clatter of their wooden shoes on the clean-swept gravel had eerie, otherworldly overtones. It was easy to believe that the god was actually present.

Because of its particularly sacred character, the renewal of the Ise shrine is not typical. Most of the other Shinto celebrations are extremely lively and colorful, attracting tourists from all over Japan and even from abroad. The Gion Festival in Kyoto, for example, lasts for almost a month, and makes cheerful even the oppressive heat of a Kyoto summer. For weeks before the processions of the 17th and 24th of July one hears from second-story windows and back alleys the *kon-chiki-chin* rhythms of bells and flutes as musicians practice for the event. The sacred car of the Gion Shrine is washed in the Kamo River, and archways are erected along the main streets. The little boy who is chosen as the *chigo,* to dance on the first of the floats, is treated like a prince for a week, and waited on by eminent dignitaries. On the night of the 16th of July, immense crowds throng the streets, dressed mainly in summer kimonos, eager to inspect the *hoko* (elaborate, steepled wagons which carry the musicians) and the *yama* (floats) which will take part in the next day's procession. The people of central Kyoto throw open their houses to everyone—literally, for the front of a Japanese house is easily removed. The *hoko* and *yama* are surrounded by clouds of white Japanese lanterns, and in front of each house on the block which provides the *hoko* or *yama* hangs an inscribed lantern.

On the following day, usually in blazing, broiling heat, the procession winds its way slowly through the streets. The *hoko* are pulled by crews of laborers directed with waving fans and rhythmical chanting by men standing at the front of the chariots. The *yama* are borne on the shoulders of grunting, sweating porters. Both the *hoko* and *yama* are swathed in superb brocades and tapestries, some of them Gobelins; the sun glinting on the gold thread makes them an unforgettable sight. The *hoko* move in stately fashion through the narrow streets, their steeples tottering dangerously at every turn in the road. From time to time the musicians throw charms wrapped in bamboo leaves to the crowd, and even in the heat people scramble to get them. The floats are decorated with life-sized figures representing heroes of Japanese and Chinese history and legends in characteristic poses. The Gion Festival was first held in 869 A.D. Judging from surviving records, it is performed today much as it was centuries ago.

The Gion Festival is the most spectacular in Japan, but it lacks some of the boisterous high spirits which make other festivals—like the Fire Festival at Kurama (near Kyoto)—even more exciting to watch. Beginning at about eleven at night, the villagers set up burning brands at regular intervals along the streets, and soon small children, shouldering flaming torches, are prancing by, piping *saireya sairyo,* the magical, meaningless refrain of the festival. Babies carried on their fathers' backs clutch miniature torches, and every size of child has a torch to match, until the boy of sixteen or seventeen carries a man's, weighing 150 pounds or more, incredible as this may seem. As the night deepens, the streets are filled with flames and smoke as drunken torchbearers, clad only in loincloths, stagger along the streets to the rhythm of *saireya sairyo,* sometimes deliberately shaking sparks into the crowd, often dangerously teetering next to the flimsy houses. Gradually the center of attention moves to the mountain behind the town: it is time for the god to make his descent. The cries of *saireya sairyo* reach a frenzied pitch as the half-naked men and women go lurching at breakneck pace down the steps through the crowd. At their destination, the god's "traveling place," innumerable burning brands illuminate the sacred dancing.

The solemn beauty of Ise, the splendid pageantry of Gion, and the intoxicating excitement of the Fire Festival typify the different qualities found in Shinto celebrations all over Japan. Almost any day in Kyoto one can see a festival, though sometimes its chief attraction may only be a horde of little boys carrying a *mikoshi* (portable shrine) and chanting *waisho, waisho,* in the time-honored way. Sometimes two festivals take place on the same day, and the two *mikoshi* "fight" as they cross. As one watches the shrine-bearers high-spiritedly tossing the *mikoshi* up into the air, one understands why a youth who has never had the chance to carry one feels permanently cheated. The fact that a young man participates in a festival does not mean that he is devoutly serving the god or even that he is undergoing a religious experience; he is there for the fun. Nevertheless, it is said that even in his roistering he may feel the god's presence.

The traditional divinities of the Shinto pantheon, such as Amaterasu (the Sun Goddess) or Takamimusubi (the Creator God), are not the object of much religious fervor today. The shrine at Ise draws large crowds, it is true, but the scenery seems to be the chief attraction. The Shinto priesthood has become a hereditary profession. It is almost unthinkable that a young man born outside the profession would wish to become a priest because of piety. There are still some devout believers in Shinto, but the religion has always been a community activity, and when (as now) the state does not support it, Shinto is weak.

Greater fervor is aroused instead in the various offshoots of Shinto and by the new religions. At the Inari Festival in Fushimi (south of Kyoto), for example, one can see people carried away by a true religious ecstasy. This festival honors the Fox God, bringer of prosperity, to whom businessmen pray for good fortune during the ensuing year. The collection boxes, which normally know only the clink of small copper coins, are filled this day with bills of large denominations, and the clapping of hands before the shrine sounds like applause.

Another prosperous religious sect is Tenri, a nineteenth-century development in Shinto with Buddhist elements. A whole town in Nara Prefecture is given over to the headquarters of this sect, and magnificent buildings, erected by the voluntary labor of the faithful, bear witness to the living importance of this religion at a time when other shrines and temples throughout the country are falling into disrepair.

58 A very small boy and a very large temple door.

KEN HEYMAN: RAPHO GUILLUMETTE

59

HORACE BRISTOL

60   SHELDON A. BRODY

61

Innumerable small, less reputable Shinto sects have sprung up during the past half-century, especially since 1945. Some of them have merely been devices which enabled unscrupulous "leaders" to extort money from gullible believers; a few have developed into nation-wide organizations.

Shinto retains its importance even today, in a time of relative adversity for the faith. The newborn baby is still presented at the local shrine to be accepted as a member of the clan (*ujiko*); a wedding most often takes place before the Shinto gods; prayers are addressed to the gods when fields are planted or crops harvested; and whatever feelings of awe and wonder are evoked by the mountainous beauty of the country are channelled into Shinto worship. Most important, perhaps, Shinto remains the national religion of Japan even when all its official connections with the state have been severed. The gods of Shinto are, after all, uniquely Japanese gods, and the religion itself a bond linking all Japanese. There is no Japanese who cannot claim to be a descendant of the gods, and no foreigner who can. A Japanese may hate Buddhism or Christianity, but it is hard for him to hate anything so intimately connected with his country as Shinto. Even the outspoken atheist delights in the Shinto festivals. However weak Shinto may now appear, it holds this attraction; future national leaders, if they so choose, may put its latent power to their own uses.

59 On the anniversary of a parent's or grandparent's death, or in memory of ancestors, prayers are written on thin slips of wood. At the entrance to the Kiyomizu Temple in Kyoto, the slips form a prayer wheel.

BUDDHISM

When Buddhism was introduced to Japan by Korean priests at the end of the sixth century, it was not only a far more complex and satisfying religion than Shinto, but it also was the vehicle which brought the great civilizations of India and China to Japan. As the first world religion it had spread in all directions from its place of origin in northern India, and raised splendid temples and monasteries in great cities and in the desert oases of Central Asia. The most brilliant men of a dozen countries had devoted themselves to compiling volumes of explanations of the sacred texts, and a prodigal outpouring of painting and sculpture filled innumerable halls and grottoes. It is not surprising that the Japanese rulers, accustomed only to the unadorned, rustic shrines of Shinto, a religion which at the time could not boast a single line of scripture, were overawed by Buddhism and eagerly sought to acquire a grasp of its principles.

60–61 People may pray before the altar inside a temple, or may stand outside and direct their prayers over the collection box to the images inside.

Buddhist texts were a medium of instruction in the Chinese language, a knowledge of which unlocked for the Japanese, still living under primitive conditions, the treasury of learning of the world's most highly civilized people. Just as many centuries later Japanese were to attend Christian churches and listen to sermons in English as a means of improving their linguistic abilities, so their ancestors in the seventh century eagerly conned Buddhist writings for help with their Chinese. Shinto, the old religion, was cast into the shade, and by the middle of the seventh century there was an emperor who "honored the religion of Buddha and despised the Way of the Gods."

The Buddhism originally introduced to Japan was a religion of monks who devoted themselves to an intensive study of extremely difficult texts. Such philosophical and theological studies had a long history in India and China, but in Japan, where the ability to read was itself a recent acquisition, it was still much too early to hope for real understanding of the sacred books. A handful of learned men in the monasteries pondered such doctrines as the dialectics of negation or the metaphysics of the harmonious whole, but only a few relatively simple ideas reached the lay Buddhists of the seventh and eighth centuries. Chief of these was the obligation of the ruler to honor and practice the Buddhist law. The piety of the court was most often expressed in the erection of temples honoring the Buddha. The city of Nara, the capital of Japan in the eighth century, is still dominated by the halls of worhip and pagodas first raised at that time. The most famous single monument of Nara Buddhism was the Great Image of Buddha, completed in 749 A.D. This bronze statue, over fifty feet in height, is still impressive, though hopelessly disfigured by earthquakes and other disasters.

Many varieties of Buddhism were introduced during the following centuries. From the ninth to the twelfth centuries esoteric teachings predominated. These purported to be doctrines of so lofty a nature that they could only be transmitted by a teacher directly to his chosen pupils. The words, bodily attitude and mind of the worshipper, all had to be attuned to this demanding religion by the recitation of sacred spells, the performance of ritual gestures, and a concentration on the mysteries of the faith. Only initiates could hope to comprehend the full glories of esoteric Buddhism, though works of art could suggest the meaning of the faith to larger numbers of believers. Court ladies used fans painted with scenes from the sacred books in order to cool themselves and derive spiritual benefit at the same time. It became fashionable for members of the aristocracy to "leave the world" as priests and nuns; however, in the interests of beauty—the passionate concern of the age—only the tips of a nun's locks were trimmed instead of her head being shaved in the required way. The Buddhism of the time was suitable to a society in which aesthetic considerations were paramount, and bad taste the most unforgivable sin.

As yet Buddhism held no appeal for the common people. From time to time the court encouraged Buddhist worship in the homes or ordered the erection of temples in the distant countryside, but the Shinto gods were much closer to the people than Buddha and his bodhisattvas living in their foreign-looking temples. Even had the ordinary folk wished to gain enlightenment, they could not have easily gone along with the Nara monks in believing that the outer world was a mere creation of the mind, nor could they have hoped to be accepted as chosen disciples of the esoteric faith.

During the twelfth century almost incessant warfare, earthquakes, and other natural disasters led to the appearance of a new type of Buddhism, one destined to win the allegiance of the vast majority of Japanese. This was the Pure Land Buddhism. It taught that the world had entered its last degenerate days and that men could no longer achieve salvation by their own efforts. Only by imploring the help of Amida, an incarnation of Buddha who had once vowed to save all men, was it possible to be reborn in paradise after death. All that was necessary was to call on Amida with the single phrase *Namu Amida Butsu*. Early missionaries spread this teaching to remote villages by dancing through the streets singing the saving invocation. Anyone could understand and practice this kind of Buddhism. It gave the ordinary farmer as great a chance of salvation as the most learned monk, or perhaps an even greater one: some adherents of Pure Land Buddhism went so far as to claim that a wicked man would be saved sooner than a priest, because a priest was likely to take a false pride in the importance of his own merits, whilst the wicked (or ignorant) man had no choice but to trust in Amida. No longer was it necessary to study the sacred texts of Buddhism; a single invocation of *Namu Amida Butsu* was enough. This sounds very simple, but it meant that a man had to humble himself to the extent of admitting that he was a nonentity incapable of saving himself. Moreover, in return for Amida's grace in admitting him to the Pure Land, a man was expected to give up everything, even his life.

It made sense to people living in a world torn by disorders when a religion taught them that this world was an evil place and the only existence which counted was the one in Amida's paradise. They eagerly accepted the new religion without, however, forsaking the Shinto gods whose help they still needed. No matter how confident a farmer might be of rebirth in the Pure Land, he had to worry about his crops while on earth, and Amida promised nothing for this life. It thus came about quite naturally that the two religions, so contradictory in their tenets, were simultaneously believed in by the mass of Japanese, who found divine help in both.

The widespread adoption of Pure Land Buddhism meant that Buddhism had at last become thoroughly Japanese. No longer was it necessary to study Sanskrit or Chinese in order to read the sacred books. The ignorant farmer could call Amida's name or sing hymns of praise written in simple Japanese. An even more pronouncedly Japanese character was lent to Buddhism by the priest Nichiren (1222–1292), who preached that Japan was the land where the true teachings of the Buddha were to be revived. His followers later claimed that Japan better deserved the name of Buddha's land than either India or China, simply because Nichiren was a Japanese. Nichiren himself rose to prominence by his repeated prophecies of disaster, which seemed confirmed in the worst way when the Mongol invasions menaced Japan at the end of the thirteenth century. He taught the importance of enduring suffering, a doctrine which his followers have put into practice by braving all opposition in order to propagandize their beliefs. Unlike some Buddhists who calmly endure suffering, Nichiren Buddhists actively court it. In their determination that their faith shall prevail, they constantly try to "break and subdue" members of other sects. Even today one may often hear late at night the beat of a drum and voices crying *Namu Myoho Renge-kyo* (Hail to the Lotus Sutra), the invocation preferred by Nichiren's followers. In the 1930's Nichiren priests frequently associated themselves with ultranationalistic movements, thus carrying their righteous determination to the field of political action. Their names still figure prominently in committees organized to "restore" Japan by re-establishing the old virtues. The martial character of Nichiren Buddhism has made it congenial to Japanese men of action.

Another type of Buddhism which originally drew its strength from the samurai class was Zen, a sect destined to exert a much wider influence than Nichiren Buddhism. Zen placed emphasis on discipline and meditation at every moment in the believer's life. The Zen masters did not abandon the sacred texts of Buddhism, as is sometimes stated, but insisted instead that they were there to be used. The believer had to lead the life of the Buddha, and the texts could help him in this. One sect of Zen developed a technique of presenting students with problems which could not be solved by ordinary logical processes, but required a flash of insight which might lead to enlightenment. The priest sitting for hours in meditation might also be startled into such an awakening by a sudden blow. But Dôgen (1200–1253), the greatest of the Zen masters, taught that obtaining sudden enlightenment was not the important thing; sitting in meditation itself could lead to a gradual and complete realization of the Buddha-nature within each man.

The insistence of Zen doctrine on self-reliance put it at opposite poles from the Pure Land sects. The place of honor in Zen temples was shared by the Buddha with images of the Zen masters of the past, ordinary men who by their own powers had realized their Buddha-nature. Zen's appeal for the military dictators of Japan in the thirteenth and fourteenth centuries was such that it developed from a discipline to a major religion with huge monasteries and properties. Many of them survive today, splendid clusters of temple buildings and gardens which are marked by a bare simplicity and cleanliness natural in those who must lead the lives of the Buddha at every moment. The severity of the Zen monastery had its equivalent in many arts: in landscape gardening, where some famous gardens (notably those of the Ryoanji and Daitokuji temples in Kyoto) consist entirely of stones and sand, as if growing plants would be an unnecessary and untidy embellishment; in the Nô theater, where all plays take place against the same backdrop of a single painted pine, and the props are no more than stylized renderings of the objects portrayed; in landscape painting, where monochromes took the place of the brilliantly colored

62 *A Christian monk of the Trappist order—in which speech is forbidden—makes the sign for "night".*

63 *Teenagers praying in a Catholic church.*

98

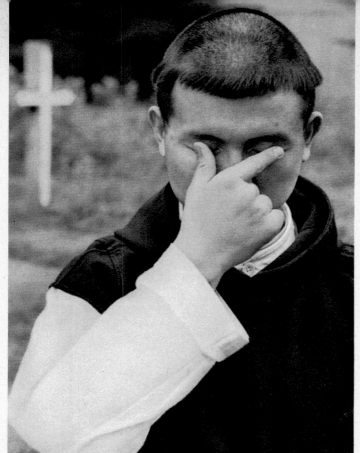

62   Kazutaka Narahara: Chuokoron-sha

63

Japanese Consulate General, New York

64

65

images favored by artists of earlier schools of Buddhism; and in the tea ceremony, an art which was almost entirely developed by Zen monks. In each of
these arts the essentials, the bare bones, are what matter, just as in Zen doctrine
realization of the Buddha-nature rather than the quiddities of theology was
emphasized. There is deliberate understatement, reflecting not the poverty of
minds which lack the imagination to handle a variety of rich effects but the
discipline of those which reject a profusion of ornamentation in favor of a few
significant lines.

Everything is controlled by the Zen adept. The Nô actor (whose walk,
incidentally, is modelled on that of the Zen priest) holds himself on guard like
a swordsman throughout the performance; it is related how an actor, taken
to task for having dropped his guard momentarily, replied that at that instant
he had been distracted by noticing a particle of dust on the stage. Dôgen himself said as he was dying, "I drop into the afterworld still living"—meaning
that he remained in control even at such a moment.

It sometimes happens, however, that when long meditation or pondering
of problems have prepared the way, there comes a moment of insight and
understanding which transcends all rational explanation, just as in a Nô play
the precise, deliberate movements of the actor at times can symbolize an indefinable, enormous world, or the stylized gestures of the tea master produce in
the beholder something partaking of eternity.

Such moments are made possible by the disciplined preparation. It is impossible to imagine, for example, a Nô actor who had never mastered the words
and movements of his performance being able to evoke the mysterious realms
of Nô symbolism by a spontaneous display of his personality. Nor could anyone who had not previously handled the implements for the tea ceremony
manage to suggest more than clumsiness. Nevertheless, a mistaken idea of what

makes for Zen in the arts has led some people in recent years to claim that their
work embodies Zen principles, and they justify their unpremeditated daubs
in terms of moments of sheer inspiration. Zen has strongly influenced many
Japanese arts, particularly those which developed between the thirteenth and
sixteenth centuries, but never as an excuse for uncontrolled "inspiration."

The Japanese Buddhist sects, despite their wide differences in doctrine, have
generally—with the notable exception of Nichiren's sect—managed to get
along amicably. Most Japanese, in any case, have only a rudimentary grasp of
the complexities of their particular sect of Buddhism. In some parts of the
country, for example, the rural population is registered mainly with Zen
temples as the result of the command issued by some local potentate centuries
ago. For most of these Zen believers, however, sitting in meditation would
be as unthinkable as performing a mass would be for the lay Catholic. Their
only connection with the temple to which they belong comes from the necessity of holding memorial services for the dead. The priest of the temple him-

self, though he undoubtedly once concerned himself with Zen doctrines, is more likely now to be preoccupied by parish activities or by the affairs of his own household. This does not mean that he is a bad priest, but that the discipline expected of a true Zen monk cannot be observed by a parish priest.

Virtually all Japanese are Buddhists, at least in name, but few young people possess any knowledge of their religion. The devotion seems to have petered out which as late as the 1890's impelled thousands of women to offer their hair to make a cable 360 feet long and strong enough to lift the timbers of the new Eastern Honganji Temple in Kyoto. Children today are barely taught to distinguish between Shinto shrines (where they must clap their hands at the altar) and Buddhist temples (where they bow in silence). With a handful of exceptions, the young men who today elect to become Buddhist priests are the sons of other priests and have decided that the priesthood offers them the best chance of making a living. There are universities in Tokyo and Kyoto established by the various Buddhist sects to train men for the priesthood, but the students tend to be resigned to their careers rather than eager.

A few young men, however, are genuinely desirous of becoming priests, and this is a hopeful sign for Buddhism. Little in Japanese life encourages them if they have a religious bent. For hundreds of years Japanese intellectuals have been attacking the Buddhist priesthood as lazy and incompetent, often with considerable justice. The popular writers of today are apt to decry religion as an "opiate of the masses," and an identification is invariably made between Buddhism and superstition. Many young priests are ashamed of their calling and wear Western clothes whenever possible, clamping felt hats on their shaven heads to conceal their identity.

A traveler arriving in Japan today from other Buddhist nations—Ceylon, Thailand or Burma—cannot but be struck by the religious apathy. Unlike the prime ministers of those countries, Japanese statesmen do not proclaim their Buddhist piety, nor do they refer to the teachings of Buddha in their public addresses. The achievements of the great Japanese Buddhist teachers have been deleted from textbooks, and the secular nature of Japanese education is stressed. Even the names of the principal sects are unknown to many university students. Nor does Buddhism retain its former hold on the farmers. In Southeast Asia enormous crowds of devout believers will eagerly press forward for a glimpse of any holy relics displayed; in Japan farmer-pilgrims are likely to be sightseers in the temples, shepherded from one "national treasure" to the next. Some writers and artists still treat Buddhist themes in their works, but usually as outsiders looking on with friendly curiosity rather than with the conviction of believers. The apathy extends to the monasteries, originally built to hold a hundred or more priests but now housing a mere five or six; in the evening the monks are more likely to gather around a television set than to read the holy books. Thanks to various dispensations of the 1870's the visitor arriving at some great temple in Kyoto may be just in time to see the butcher present his weekly bill, or he may interrupt a priest playing with his children. It is small wonder that travelers from Southeast Asia, where meat-eating, married priests are inconceivable, refuse to believe that the Japanese are really Buddhists.

Most Buddhist temples in Japan are today in poor economic shape. The land reforms after 1945 deprived them of the chief source of their income. Today the larger temples depend in part on the admission fees charged for the privilege of examining their treasures. The central temples of a sect also receive contributions from each of the affiliated temples throughout the country. Rich men are sometimes persuaded to contribute to fund-raising drives; one sees their names and the amount they have given written on signs outside the temples. The situation is much worse in remote temples, where sometimes it is impossible to find a successor when the old priest dies. Temples in scenic spots have taken to renting their premises for meetings and picnics or even serve as hotels. Other temples, less likely to attract tourists, have become lodgings for poor students, or hang signs at their gates announcing that lessons in calligraphy or flower arrangement can be arranged. The gardens of such temples are likely to be overgrown, the paintings on the paper screens peeling and discolored, and weeds three feet high grow from the tops of the gates. The casual visitor is stared at by small children in the courtyard, and when the priest's wife appears from the kitchen in an apron she timidly asks for the entrance fee. If anything commends the temple, she will have memorized the description from some old guidebook, and as she leads the visitor through the dilapidated rooms to reach some statue or painting, she hastily shuts doors on rooms where clothes are being mended or bedding still lies on the floor.

Temples are generally deserted except during the Bon festival in August and while funeral services are actually in progress. Some temples have annual festivals, but they differ from Shinto festivals in that they are spectacles, and not celebrations in which the crowd may join. The Nigatsu-do (Hall of the Second Moon), a temple in Nara, actually has a stage where the priests perform at *Mizutori,* "the water-dipping." This ancient ceremony was originally a mass confessional of the priests, but today it features weird "Tartar" dances and ritual. A crowd of spectators surrounds the hall, peering through lattice-work windows at the priests who pass by circling the main altar in the semi-darkness, chanting spells in a mysterious language, and pounding with their wooden shoes on the floor boards. Bashô described it:

Mizutori ya	Water-dipping rite—
Kôri no sô no	The clatter of the pattens
Kutsu no oto	Of the cloistered priests.

It is a haunting sight to see the priests, clad in Central-Asian robes, performing their incantations in the flickering torchlight. At the conclusion they rush forward onto the temple stage and dance to wild rhythms swinging great brands and showering cascades of sparks on the spectators below. The water-dipping is now a relatively minor part of the ceremony, though once the sacred water was believed to be a magical elixir.

The Buddhist ceremonial in which the public takes the greatest part is the Bon festival, a kind of Feast of the Dead held in August. Most Japanese, wherever they may reside, go back to their ancestral home at least for this one occasion to decorate the family graves with flowers. The dead are said to return at this season, and a visit to the graves is therefore especially important. In some villages along the coast the souls of the dead are sent away after the festival in tiny boats bearing lights that disappear at sea.

Everywhere in Japan there are Bon dances. One may see them in empty lots in the cities, where a scratchy phonograph record blasts out the musical accompaniment over loudspeakers, and the dancers wear sport shirts and printed summer frocks. In the country, especially in a remote region like the Valley of Kiso, the dances preserve something of the traditions of the past. At dusk the people begin to gather in the main street of the town, forming a circle. All wear Japanese dress, or at least elements of it, and tie a towel around their head. One person takes up the refrain, a somewhat bawdy ballad, and the dancers perform to it the four or five simple movements of the dance. The burden of the song passes from one man or woman to another, and gradually the circle of dancers grows larger, until the whole town seems to be dancing under the bright August moon.

Little in the Bon festival dances suggests their Buddhist origins, and some scholars even assert that they are completely secular. Japanese tend to think of Buddhism as a gloomy religion of the dead, but the liveliness of these dances accords poorly with this belief.

Buddhism, for all its present decline, has indelibly colored the Japanese way of thinking. For example, the impermanence of this world, perhaps the most frequently reiterated theme in Buddhist writings, gave rise to the peculiarly Japanese concept of beauty. The priest Kenkô wrote in the fourteenth century, "Were we to live on forever, then indeed would men not feel the pity of things. Truly the beauty of life is its uncertainty." The Japanese came to prize perishability, a trait which Lafcadio Hearn once termed "the genius of Japanese civilization." He wrote, in *Kokoro,* "Generally speaking, we construct for endurance, the Japanese for impermanency. Few things for common use are made in Japan with a view to durability. The straw sandals worn out and replaced at each stage of a journey; the robe consisting of a few simple widths loosely stitched together for wearing, and unstitched again for washing; the fresh chopsticks served to each new guest at a hotel; the light *shoji* frames serving at once for windows and walls, and repapered twice a year; the matting renewed every

66–67 Although Buddhist nuns shave their heads and have such duties as praying, conducting ceremonies, and cleaning temples, there is room for gaiety.

66   WERNER BISCHOF: MAGNUM

67

TADAHIKO HAYASHI: CHUOKORON-SHA

autumn—all these are but random examples of countless small things in daily life that illustrate the national contentment with impermanency."

To bewail the passing of things or the changes that time brings is common to many peoples and literatures (and may be found in Japan too), but to discover in impermanence the essence of beauty is characteristic of Japan. The fact that the cherry blossom is considered the Japanese national flower underlines this point. The cherry blossoms are in their glory for at most three or four days, and during the rest of the year the tree is an utter nuisance. It produces thousands of minuscule inedible cherries which must be swept away; it is such a great favorite with insects, particularly caterpillars, that by the end of summer one is well advised to carry an umbrella under its boughs; and it loses its leaves long before the other trees. Yet for a few days of enjoyment the Japanese not only tolerate the cherry tree, but plant it everywhere and genuinely love it. Indeed, if the blossoms stayed longer on the boughs (like plum blossoms, for example), the tree would undoubtedly be less highly prized because less impermanent. The Japanese soldier during the war liked to compare himself to the cherry blossoms falling after a brief moment of glory, rather than to the chrysanthemums blooming steadfastly.

Small children are taught the Buddhist lesson of impermanence. The poem from which the Japanese have traditionally learned their syllabary (it contains each of the forty-seven syllables) begins

Iro ha nihohedo	Though the color be fragrant
Chirinuru wo	The flower will fall:
Waga yo tarezo	Who in this world of ours
Tsune naramu…	Will last forever?

The child at first unthinkingly parrots the syllables, but something of the poem's content will sooner or later affect him. Not only the poem, of course, but innumerable other works of Japanese literature confirm this view of life. No matter how violently a Japanese may oppose Buddhism, he has been unalterably tinged by its philosophy, much in the way that an Italian, even an atheist, will have been by Catholicism. Because most children receive no religious instruction today, they are likely to be ignorant of everything they see in a temple. Yet they will almost instinctively appreciate the beauty of works of art which may baffle foreigners, and in their speech they inevitably have recourse to the many words which Buddhism has given the Japanese language. Tough young men today do not, it is true, blame their misfortunes on the sins of a previous existence, but they seem to share in the fatalism which is said to come from the Buddhist doctrine of *karma*.

Today the Buddhist altar is empty in some Japanese houses. In others the daily offering of cooked rice and water is neglected. But in millions of houses

68   *A komusô,* member of an order *of begging priests, goes through the streets playing a vertical flute. According to ancient custom his head is completely covered by the basket.*

107

the prescribed observances are faithfully continued, and every present received by the family is first placed before the Buddha. Carpenters have had to find ways of fitting a Buddhist altar into some of the newly built Tokyo houses, though no need for one had been anticipated by the young and up-to-date owners. Indeed, one of the most striking features of Buddhism in Japan during the past few centuries has been how close it has frequently seemed to destruction, and how each time—often for no apparent reason—it has managed to survive. When one visits some old deserted temple, where there is not even a resident priest, it is easy to visualize it crumbling into mouldering timbers as the hands of its statues drop off, and the gold leaf flakes from the altar. Yet the traveler who returns years later, expecting to find a desolate wilderness, may equally well see new tiles on the roof and fresh gilding on the images. The Buddhist cycle, after all, insists not only on decay but regeneration.

CONFUCIANISM

During most of the period between 1600 and 1868 Confucianism enjoyed a position similar to that of a state religion. The teachings of the great Chinese sage were pondered by philosophers and statesmen who paid him homage worthy of a god. Confucian doctrine trickled down from their writings to the level of the common people. Yet this was not a religion in the normal sense. It had little to say about an afterlife—either heaven or hell--but often denied the existence of gods or other supernatural beings. The government established temples for the worship of Confucius, but as a man and not as a god.

A popular religious leader of the early nineteenth century urged his followers, "Revere Shinto, Buddhism, and Confucianism and cherish sincerity in all." A literal observance of this command obliged a man to believe simultaneously in the Shinto gods, Buddha, and in the non-existence of both; yet this contradiction did not disturb the Japanese. Confucianism meant in practice not its denials of the supernatural but its insistence on filial piety, loyalty, obligation, respect for the government, and other secular virtues.

Some of the outstanding Confucian philosophers in Japan were at the same time devout believers in the mystic qualities of the Land of the Rising Sun, and claimed that Japan exemplified the virtues of Confucius even better than China itself. Loyalty to the Emperor, for example, a tenet of Shinto, could be explained in terms of Confucian loyalty.

Confucian philosophy continued to be of great importance even after the introduction of Western science and philosophy. It became the defense of Japan as an "Eastern" country against unwanted encroachments of Western ideas. The Japanese rulers favored progress, but they did not wish to encourage any ideas of equality which might lead to changes in the existing order. The

Emperor Meiji, who had proclaimed his government's intention of seeking knowledge throughout the world, retained a Confucian scholar as his adviser, and his edicts were invariably Confucian both in language and sentiments.

Today Confucianism is no longer a religion in Japan. The few remaining Confucian shrines attract no worshippers, and only a few of the students who read Lamb's *Tales from Shakespeare* or *Treasure Island* ever turn to the writings of the Chinese sage. Yet much that is immediately recognizable as traditional in Japan may be traced to Confucianism. Man's ultimate concerns are most often expressed in Buddhist language, but the vocabulary of the social relations comes from the Confucian scholar.

CHRISTIANITY

Christianity in Japan had its inception in 1549, the year when Saint Francis Xavier arrived in Kagoshima and began his teaching. Portuguese traders had reached Japan only a few years earlier—nobody is sure of the exact date—and were the first Europeans ever to visit the country. Xavier, attracted by reports of a rich and populous country inhabited by cultivated people, resolved to carry Christianity to Japan. He was assisted by a Japanese who spoke a little Portuguese, but the difficulties of explaining Christian doctrine were far beyond the capacities of this interpreter, and Xavier often had to face ridicule. Nevertheless he persisted, and by the time he left Japan two years afterwards he had succeeded in converting about a thousand souls. Xavier referred to the Japanese as "the delight of my heart."

Thanks to the diligent efforts of Portuguese and other Catholic missionaries, by 1614 there were about 300,000 Christians in Japan. Converted Japanese potentates contributed to this large number by ordering the mass conversion of their vassals. The enthusiasm of some of these barons for Christianity was heightened by a desire to ingratiate themselves with the Portuguese and share in the lucrative trade brought by the foreign ships. It was not surprising that when the government began the persecution of Christians many who had been converted because of opportunism easily renounced the faith. What is remarkable, however, is the extraordinary devotion which many others showed to their religion. Between 1614 and 1640, close to 6,000 Japanese became martyrs under circumstances of incredible suffering. The tortures devised to make the Christians give up their faith were so horrible that burning at the stake came to be considered a mild punishment.

The government was determined to stamp out Christianity because it feared that Christian missionary activity might in Japan, as elsewhere in Asia, be the prelude to colonial expansion. It feared also that foreigners might support Christian barons in case of a rebellion. The English and Dutch traders in Japan, enemies of the Portuguese both in religion and commerce, encouraged the Japanese in these beliefs. Dissension among the different groups of Catholic missionaries also helped to weaken the Christian cause. Nevertheless, despite the terrible tortures meted out to every Christian who was discovered, many joyfully became martyrs. As part of the same anti-Christian campaign the government required every Japanese to be affiliated with a Buddhist temple, and people were regularly required to demonstrate their anti-Christianity by trampling on metal images of the Virgin and Child. These precautions continued long after the government could have suspected that any Christians were left in Japan.

It came as an immense surprise to everyone in 1865 when several thousand Catholics confessed themselves to a French priest in Nagasaki. Their families had been secretly practicing Christianity for over two hundred years, knowing that the treachery of a single person would bring death to the others. They had used in their worship images of the Virgin disguised as the Buddhist deity Kwannon, and the cross ingeniously worked into heraldic designs. One can imagine their emotions on at last meeting a priest of their own faith.

But if they supposed that their long sufferings were at an end, they were much mistaken: the anti-Christian laws were still in effect, and hundreds were quickly arrested. In 1869 the government ordered all Christians near Nagasaki to be seized, and three thousand of them were sent to remote parts of the country where they were subjected to the cruelest tortures in the hope of making them recant. The prohibition on Christianity was not lifted until 1873.

Even before then, however, European and American doctors and teachers had secretly begun to give instruction in Christianity to their pupils. Bible classes led to conversions, and before long some of the most earnest and progressive young men in the nation were devout Christians.

For many Japanese the great attraction of Christianity was the fact that it was the faith of the West. They were trying in every way to emulate the West, and this led them to believe that acquiring its religion would help make Japan a better and stronger nation. In the 1880's, when the revival movement was at its height, thousands joined the church. At times the Protestant missionaries believed that the conversion of the whole nation was in sight, but they underestimated the strength of the opposition. Sometimes Christianity came into direct conflict with a man's patriotic duties, as was dramatized when Uchimura Kanzô (1861–1930), a leading Christian, was expelled from his teaching post because he refused to bow when the Imperial Rescript on education was read aloud. This conflict continued until the outbreak of the Greater East Asia War in 1941, leading at times to uneasy compromises, at times to bitter dispute. Some converts, who had believed that Christianity stood for unwavering principles, were disillusioned by factionalism among the different Protestant denominations, or by theological controversies over evolution and other new theories.

69 *As part of the celebration at a country wedding in Niigata, the children beat the bridegroom with wooden swords.*

70 *Evil influences are chased away from the bride by the priest's wand. Although most Japanese are Buddhists, wedding ceremonies are almost always held according to Shinto ritual.*

71 *The bride drinks three cups of saké, the most important moment of the wedding ceremony.*

69

70

71

The growth of Christianity slowed down markedly after its spectacular progress in the 1880's, and though it succeeded in gaining recognition as one of the three religions of Japan, even the most optimistic missionary no longer thought that the conversion of the nation was in sight.

The 1914–1918 War disillusioned still other Japanese with the ideals of the West and impeded the spread of Christianity. Young men who had turned to the religion for its social message, its works for the poor, and its concern with suffering, found greater appeal in socialism and other political programs.

Protestant missionaries had concentrated on the Japanese leaders in the hope that converting a single one of them would bring over a thousand men, but many of these leaders proved fickle and dropped their religion when it became inconvenient. Even those who remained faithful were unable to win over the vast uneducated masses to a religion presented in terms with so little emotional appeal. The tendency of many Japanese Protestants to prefer a "non-church" Christianity meant that even if they themselves continued to read the Bible and say their prayers, their children, lacking the guidance of an organized religion, often did not follow them. In comparison, the Catholics, especially around their old stronghold of Nagasaki, continued to demonstrate a religious fervor which seemed to justify their policy of propagating their faith among the common people.

The Japanese defeat of 1945 and the subsequent Allied Occupation brought about a new wave of adulation for the West, one less critical even than the pro-Westernism of the 1880's. Democratic institutions were exalted in place of the old authoritarian ways, and Americanism, whether in the form of election campaigns or chewing gum, was insanely popular. Christianity, not surprisingly, enjoyed a fresh spurt of popularity. Japanese girls who fell in love with American servicemen became Christians, and other Japanese felt that they could only atone for their war guilt by religious devotions. The Supreme Commander of the Allied Forces, General Douglas MacArthur, confided to some missionaries that if he so desired he could bring about the conversion of the entire nation. Rumors had it that the Emperor and the Imperial Family were shortly to be baptized. The religiously-minded Occupation authorities for a time permitted no foreign books except religious tracts to be imported, and missionaries were the only foreigners allowed into the country. But the Christianization order never was issued; the Emperor remained a worshipper of the Sun Goddess; and many of those who had eagerly embraced the religion of the admirable Americans stopped going to church.

Christianity today fills a prominent but not very important place in Japanese life. Churches dot the cities and parts of the countryside—Gothic, Victorian and New England in architecture. Christian universities are popular though only a small part of the students are Christians, and there are not many conversions. Only about half of one per cent of the population is Christian. Nevertheless,

72 Huge floats are pulled through the narrow streets of Kyoto during the Gion Festival. Musicians ride upstairs; below, men use fans to direct the crews tugging the float.

Christmas Eve is widely celebrated in the cities—as an occasion to go to night-clubs. Santa Claus has been imported to Japan, and many non-Christian households are graced by Christmas trees. In Nagasaki, the one city with a markedly Christian character, dolls dressed as nuns are sold in the railway station souvenir stalls for the benefit of people from other parts of the country who desire this exotic touch. Crucifixes make popular souvenirs.

One of the chief obstacles to the widespread adoption of Christianity has been its exclusiveness. If Christianity had been content like Buddhism, Shinto or Confucianism with only a share of the Japanese religious life, it might have obtained it. It insisted, however, that Japanese Christians might not join their fellow countrymen in bowing their heads before the gods, and that they must not be buried in accordance with the customs of their ancestors. The Japanese therefore had to choose between all or nothing. Some chose to give all. Japanese have eagerly become Trappist monks, and live by a discipline which is possibly severer than that of Trappists elsewhere.

Not all aspects of Japanese Christianity are attractive. It sometimes leads to an excessive fondness for the company of foreigners and the adoption of unsuitable mannerisms such as a hollow-sounding heartiness. Sometimes it leads to a mousey piety very distressing to non-Japanese Christians. But being a Christian in an overwhelmingly non-Christian country is an affirmation and a responsibility, as many Japanese realize, and they have displayed at times a rare intensity of faith. The Nagasaki doctor, himself a victim of atomic radiation, who spent the last years of his life caring for other victims, lived in a house so tiny that there was barely room for himself and the statue of the Virgin which was his comfort. Other Christians, like the famous Dr. Toyohiko Kagawa, have won world recognition.

The promise of a Christian Japan seems less close to achievement now than it did in the 1880's. Many of those now carrying on leftist political activity are in fact the heirs of the ideals of the "non-church" movement, though they may be professionally anti-religious. Missionaries still labor in all parts of the country, sometimes with great devotion but seldom with conspicuous results. They now have counterparts in the Japanese Buddhist missionaries preaching in the United States; if anything, the latter seem to be creating more excitement.

RELIGION AND SUPERSTITION

It is obviously difficult to distinguish between religion and superstition, though many people have made the attempt. How to classify, for example, the numerous cults which sprang up in Japan after the war, headed by outlandishly garbed wizards and priestesses? Or when do practices of an established religion like Shinto—such as the prohibition on the planting of watermelons because they

are offensive to a local god—forfeit respectability and become mere superstition? In 1946, when the government of a new democratic Japan established
a committee for the investigation and control of superstitions, it decided to
treat as superstition all manner of divination, fortune-telling, magical cures and
curses, as well as ghosts, apparitions and possessive demons. For a time the
government forbade the publication of astrological almanacs which listed lucky
and unlucky days, "prohibited directions" and other lore from the dim past,
but they are now sold again to millions of people anxious, in the old phrase, to
"avoid calamity."

Every village has its own superstitions, though most are shared with other
communities in Japan. Many originated in China, particularly in the *yin-yang*
system of thought. Practitioners of *yin-yang* would indignantly deny that it
was superstition; for centuries there was an established department of *yin-yang*
divination in the Japanese government, and even in our day the marriage date
of the Crown Prince was decided by these methods. *Yin-yang* was originally
a kind of science based on the principle that there are correspondences among
the five elements, the five planets, the five directions (including the center), the
colors, the organs of the body, the seasons, and so on. The twelve signs of the
zodiac were also apportioned among the five elements. Thus, the planet Jupiter
corresponded to the element Wood, the direction East, the season Spring, the
color green, and the signs of the zodiac the Tiger and the Hare. A person born
under this sign could "avoid calamity" by marrying someone born under the
planets Mars or Mercury, but not under Saturn or Venus. Certain days would
be unlucky for him because of conjunctions of the stars, and there were also
forbidden directions. As late as the 1946 poll, forty per cent of those questioned
believed that the sign of the zodiac a man was born under determined his
personality. Some seventy-three per cent believed in lucky and unlucky days, and
the percentage of belief was even higher for *tomobiki*—days on which the performance of an auspicious or unlucky action will involve other people in
similar actions. Of course people nowadays often follow such superstitions less
out of conviction than in deference to the customs of their community.

The number of superstitions is limitless. For example, a sociologist has listed
thirty commonly held superstitions about death in one small locality alone,
including: if you stumble on the way to a funeral, somebody else will die in
your family; if a bird sings on the roof of a Buddhist temple, somebody will
die; if you feel sleepier than usual, it means a relative will die. Various other
superstitions are: if you slice a melon at night you won't be present when your
parents die; if a pregnant woman sees a hare, her child will be born with a
hare-lip; if you go to bed immediately after eating, you'll turn into an ox.
Such superstitions are by no means confined to the people of former times or
to the ignorant countryfolk today. The streetcars in Kyoto carry prominent
advertisements (paid for by the municipal transit system) advising riders which

years are "ill-omened" in a man's or woman's life, and suggesting temples where they may be freed of the curse. A man who buys a house in Tokyo today should not be surprised if the previous owner begs for another month in the house so that he will not have to move in an unlucky direction. The Japanese are also superstitious about numbers, particularly the numbers four and forty-two, which are homophones for the word meaning "death." There are no rooms with those numbers in hospitals. Even in such expressions as "four o'clock" or "four men" one uses another pronunciation for the word "four" so as not to suggest death.

Superstition takes a different form with the fortune-tellers, physiognomists, palm-readers and other purveyors of the future. Most of them flourish in little booths along the streets decorated with weird symbols and diagrams. The fortune-tellers claim that their knowledge is derived from the ancient Chinese classic *The Book of Changes,* and many of them accordingly affect Chinese dress or allow their beards and nails to grow long. Everyone has heard of fortune-tellers whose predictions are marvelously accurate, but most Japanese treat these diviners with the same mixture of credulity and suspicion that people in the West give to gypsies. It does not appear to be a lucrative profession.

The supernatural, however, need not be purchased—ghosts and apparitions brighten the lives of many Japanese. The true ghost may be distinguished by the absence of feet, and is almost invariably a woman. The long black locks hanging over a shroud are indeed a chilling sight—so much so that in the summertime ghost plays take the place of air conditioning in many theaters! Foxes, badgers, snakes and other animals frequently assume human form or become terrifying apparitions. The fertile imagination of artists and writers have provided us with a grand gallery of monsters—headless horrors, heads that move without bodies, creatures with one eye, legs that walk by themselves. Among the most famous of these fantastic creatures are *kappa,* childlike water sprites with faces like tigers, sharp bills, scales on their hairless bodies, and a dent in the crown of their heads. They are believed to cause children to drown by luring them into rivers, but are nevertheless considered to be genial and amusing. The *tengu*—red-faced, long-nosed, winged creatures—are believed to haunt the mountains. Like the *kappa* their comic appearance gives them a popularity denied to run-of-the-mill devils and goblins.

Very few people still actually believe in the existence of such monsters, though ghost stories are common enough. There is one supernatural phenomenon which many Japanese claim to have seen—the *hitodama,* a ball of fire said to emanate from a dying person's body and afterwards to hover like a will-o'-the-wisp in the sky. Sceptics discount such reports and say that *hitodama* are shooting stars, fireflies or birds.

Many superstitions are found on the fringes of the recognized religions. For example, some people believe that a good way to cure diseases of the eye is

73   *The past comes to life again at a Shinto festival in Fukushima: solemn warriors in medieval armor bear banners dyed with their families' crests.*

74   *(Over) Naked revellers carry a* mikoshi *(portable shrine) of a Shinto god.*

75   *(Over) Sometimes two* mikoshi *from different directions meet in wild turmoil, as here at the "Fight Festival" held each October in Himeji.*

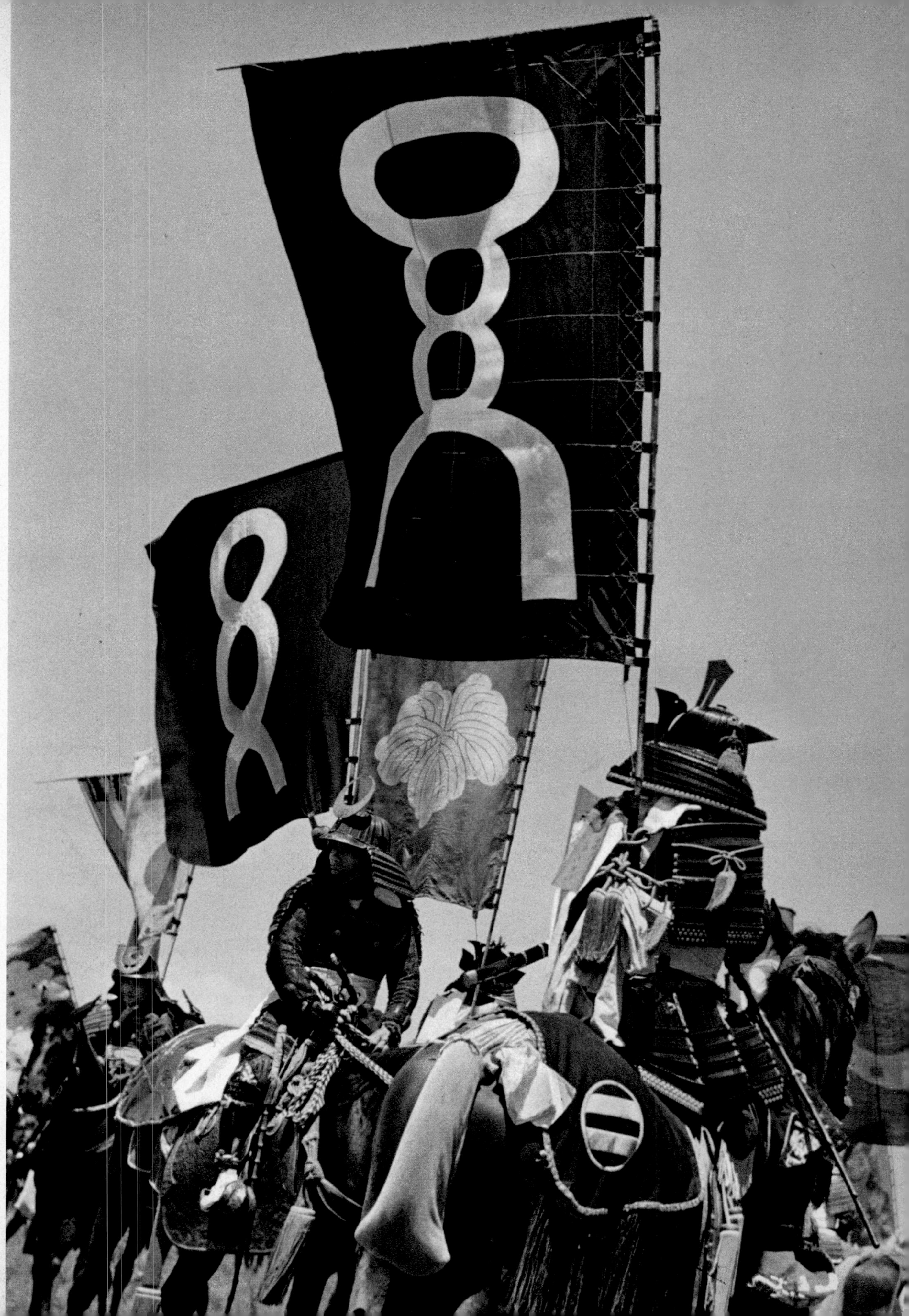

Hiroshi Hamaya

74

SHELDON A. BRODY

75

first to rub the eyes of a statue of Binzuru, a Buddhist deity, and then to rub one's own afflicted eyes. This practice, of course, is more likely to spread eye disease than to cure it, and the Buddhist scriptures give no authorization for it. Prayers are offered to both Buddhist and Shinto deities for miraculous cures— to at least fourteen Buddhas and thirty-six gods. Prayers may involve such different rituals as the abstinence from certain foods and the consumption of others; the offering of votive pictures; the purchase of amulets; the pasting of charms on the kitchen wall (or framing them in little cases in the taxi or bus one drives); or the making of a hundred pilgrimages. Every malady is controlled by one or several gods and Buddhas, each of whom expects appropriate observances. In case of measles, one should pray to the Healing Buddha and eat lobster. For toothache there are two gods, one of whom must be appeased with four chopsticks, and the other of whom disapproves of people eating pears. For warts there are two Buddhas and two gods (including a Wart Buddha and a Wart God) who require such different actions as eating mud pies, offering a *torii* made of metal, or rubbing one's warts against a stone statue. Other magical cures involve no religious activity. Recommended for curing children of wetting their beds are: eating a red dog, a tree-frog, a charred mouse or a locust. For a child who cries in his sleep it may be sufficient to write the ideograph for "devil" three times and put the paper next to his pillow.

Superstition on the whole seems to be losing out in Japan. One still hears of children worshipped as divinities in the remote villages where they live; of mediums who speak in their trances with the voices of the dead; of Kokkuri-sama, a kind of ouija board; of wise women who effect miraculous cures. In numerous small ways the visitor's attention is caught by superstition. If he asks why, for example, restaurants always serve two slices of pickle, he will be told that it is because one slice (*hito-kiri*) is a homophone for "to stab somebody else" and three slices (*mi-kiri*) for "to stab oneself." If, however, one reads the accounts of travelers in the past, it will be apparent how sharply the forces of superstition have dwindled.

Religion and superstition have both suffered in the years since the war, victims of indifference rather than antagonism. The child who has grown up in the cities during this period has probably no interest in either. Those old enough to remember how they were compelled during the war to bow before Shinto shrines are not likely to recall the experience with pleasure. The government, however, has at times shown itself concerned about religion, or at least about the old morality, and it seems likely that its fate will be closely linked to political considerations.

76 Kanto *(lantern pole) festivals are held every August in Akita in northern Japan. The men compete in balancing forty-foot poles on their chins, foreheads and hips. The lanterns are inscribed with the names of advertisers—here, a fertilizer company.*

Chapter IV

FISHERMEN, FARMERS AND ASSEMBLY LINES

77 *A little boy at a festival
wears the same ancient robes as
the priests.*

THE PICTURE of Japan as a land of cherry blossoms and geishas has gained such a hold on the imagination of many Westerners that they find it hard to remember that Japan is a modern industrial nation. The man who knows as a fact that Japan exports ships, steel bars and chemicals, is nevertheless surprised to find picturesque landscapes dotted with the chimneys of huge factories. The tourist, looking out the window of his speeding, air-conditioned train, may be so affected by legends he has read of the Land of the Gods that he may wonder, when he sees farmers spraying their fields with insecticides, what magical rites are being celebrated. Japanese people traveling abroad complain they are frequently subjected to questions that reveal an inability to reconcile impressions of beauteous Japan with those of the aggressive rival for trade.

A certain amount of confusion about the Japanese economy is, however, understandable. No country presents more contradictions to the observer. Japan has become the largest shipbuilding country in the world, but unlike other industrially advanced countries, forty per cent of the population still maintain themselves primarily by agriculture, and about half of the remaining workers are either self-employed or work for their families. Again, Japan excels in the production of cameras, radios and precision instruments, evidence that the country has reached the technical level of Germany or Switzerland, yet a depressingly large part of its consumer goods is still produced in tiny, ill-lighted tenement rooms. Fast trains and airplanes link almost every corner of the country, yet one still sees ox-carts on city streets. Such a list of contrasts might be prolonged indefinitely. Each item indicates how unevenly Japanese industrialization has progressed—or at least how different it is from the pattern now established in Europe and America.

77

Of a total working population of 43 million in 1958, some 17 million were employed in agriculture and fishing, and the remaining 26 million in manufacturing, business, government offices and so on. It is frequently stated that the most serious problem facing Japan both in agriculture and industry is overpopulation. Japan is the fifth most populous country in the world and has the highest density in terms of the arable land. Many people in the West therefore imagine that the Japanese birth-rate must be astronomically high. Population experts point out, however, that the Japanese, alone of the peoples of Asia, have steadily brought down their birth-rate. It dropped from 33 per thousand in 1947 to 17.2 per thousand in 1957, and is now well below the American birth-rate. Yet even with the present modest rate of increase the pressure of population is felt with mounting intensity. The land cannot support more farmers; fishing grounds would be in danger of depletion if more fishermen put out to sea; and the managers of already over-staffed industries wonder how they can make room for the new crop of high school and college graduates. Out-and-out unemployment has not ranked as a major problem since the war, but hidden unemployment was conservatively estimated in 1951 at about twenty per cent of the working population. The high percentage is explained by the fact that so many Japanese work for their families at little or no pay in return for bare subsistence. This is true particularly in such traditional occupations as farming and fishing.

78 *Just as the cherry blossoms are opening along the northwest coast, women go to the river mouths to catch tiny fish in their hand nets.*

AGRICULTURE

Farmers have played a curiously ambiguous role in the Japanese life of the past few centuries. Confucian philosophers extolled them as the "cornerstone" of the nation's economy, and contrasted their productivity with the sinister, "weevil-like" activities of the merchants. Yet praise of the farmers was always contingent on their knowing their place, and any material improvement in their lot was sharply criticized. The news, for example, that the farmers of a certain district had taken to drinking tea excited the indignation of the very men who insisted on the dignity and excellence of the farmer's profession. The authorities not only looked with suspicion on prosperous farmers, but were likely to respond with heavier taxes. Although in the traditional social ranking farmers took precedence over artisans and merchants, this did not hold true of their material conditions. Long after rice became the usual fare for city-dwellers, farmers tasted it only on rare holidays, and during the rest of the year had to content themselves with coarse grains. Their houses, unlike the substantial dwellings of the merchants, were often mere hovels without the simplest amenities. The only break in their daily routine came with the festivals.

The harshness of the life they led is indicated by the numerous peasant revolts. Normally docile Japanese farmers, unable to bear the oppressive weight of taxes and other exactions, rebelled with mounting frequency during the Tokugawa Period (1603–1868), preferring death to their miserable lot.

The first serious shocks to the old system were brought about by the wars in which Japan engaged during the late nineteenth century. The conscript army took many farm boys away from home, and introduced them to Western clothes, food and ideas. Compulsory education also acquainted villagers with the outside world, and even those farmers who at first had opposed education began to see in it the means for a better life. Modern ideas weakened traditional beliefs in the gods and Buddhas and loosened the grip of superstition. The standard of living rose, though poverty continued to plague most farmers, who fell farther than ever behind the rapidly progressing townsmen. Infanticide, a common practice before the Restoration, died out, but girls of poor families were often sold into prostitution. Other girls, more fortunate, were sent off to the cities as badly paid factory workers and servants. The young men were liable to end up as day-laborers.

But although conditions were much worse on the farms than in the towns, mass migration to the cities was not feasible. For one thing the government discouraged it, for another the kind of agriculture practiced in Japan demanded the labor of the entire family. There was as yet little mechanisation, and in order for all the arduous work of planting and harvesting to be completed, even the small children had to help.

The first conspicuous improvement in the farmer's lot came, ironically enough, during the 1941–45 War. Although required to sell most of their crops to the government at nominal prices, what remained was an invaluable asset at a time when the entire country was suffering from a terrible food shortage. City-dwellers went out to the countryside with silk kimonos and objects of art to barter for turnips and barley. For the first time the advantage was with the farmers, and though some of them rather abused their position, few people could begrudge them this chance after centuries of misery. Their good fortune was confirmed after the war by the American-inspired land reforms, which broke up the large estates and made most tenant farmers the owners of the land which they had been cultivating. This move had the desired effect of making the farmers politically conservative, for they now possessed a stake in the existing system.

Other changes since the war have considerably lightened the farmers' burden and made life in the rural areas more agreeable. Industrialization has affected virtually every part of the country. There is electricity in even the smallest hamlets, thanks to the abundance of hydroelectric power. Ninety per cent of the houses have radios, and two thirds own sewing machines. Television aerials clutter the roofs of houses in the remote mountains. On the other hand, the number of farmers who still make their own straw matting or

79 As torches attract the trout, the cormorants dive into the river to catch them. Rings around their necks prevent them from swallowing the fish. Gifu.

80 Giant crabs are caught in the North Pacific, for domestic consumption and export. Many canneries operate at sea.

79

80

81

82

weave their own cloth has shrunk to the vanishing point, though not so long ago such handicrafts were common. In the villages people are less likely to use pottery from a local kiln than mass-produced china brought from an entirely different part of Japan. Characteristic local products are fast being replaced at tourist spots by souvenirs, identical (save for the names) to those sold at countless other places.

Conditions in the Japanese countryside have improved markedly during the past twenty or so years, despite a devastating war and its consequences. If the period of 1934–1936 be taken as the norm of 100, the level of consumption in the country rose by 1957 to 134.6. This remarkable increase was occasioned in part by the extremely low level of 1934–1936, but the improvement was genuine. The diet, for example, changed conspicuously: rice, formerly a luxury for farmers, came to be eaten regularly, and in some regions meat as well as fish often graced the farmers' table. The standard of living has risen so much that one Japanese sociologist claims that the farmers should now be considered "middle class." The life of a farmer is still hard, but there is little misery in Japan of the kind commonly seen elsewhere in Asia or in southern Europe. It comes as a surprise to Japanese (who are accustomed to thinking of their country as very poor) when they see, in some village in Spain or Italy, the terrible marks of malnutrition on the children's faces. Japanese tend to be gloomy about their country, and when, for example, they speak of the farmers they usually refer to those in the Northeast, the worst-off in the country, and not to those in the relatively prosperous West. Even in the Northeast, however, the improvement between 1947 and 1957 was startling: thanks to several years of bumper harvests, electric washing machines have made life easier for many farmers' wives, and motorcycles carry farmers to their fields. In 1947 about 8,000 small tractors were in use throughout Japan; a decade later some 300,000 farms were equipped with them. Threshing machines increased in the same period from 440,000 to 2,500,000 units, which meant that almost half of the nation's six million farms now owned such machines. Further mechanization has been hampered less by an inability to pay for machinery than by the smallness of the farms.

One sees signs of improvement everywhere in the rural areas. The village busses are filled with women in attractive clothes of good quality, instead of the shapeless body-coverings patched together from old kimono material which were formerly the rule. The village shops are filled with electrical appliances, and the streets noisy with three-wheeled trucks. Some intellectuals indeed are worried lest the farmers, seduced by this new prosperity, may think so much of material improvements that they will forget more serious issues. Not surprisingly, the farmer who has just put a new roof on his house and hears a washing machine's gentle purr in his kitchen may be disinclined to listen to prophecies of gloom. Yet each one knows in his heart that a few years of bad

81 Women dive for edible seaweed, abalones and pearls.

82 At Kujukuri on the east coast, women, who often do heavy work in Japan, pull fishing boats up on the beach.

crops—the work of typhoons or other natural disasters which man is power-less to control—may wipe out his present prosperity. Moreover, the general improvement has not affected all farmers equally. Even though the man working a tiny plot of land receives more money for his crops than ever before, he is placed increasingly at a disadvantage to the owners of bigger farms who can profit by mechanization. The gap between the wealthy farmer and the small farmer is widening, and cooperative action among the latter may be necessary if they are not to be forced into bankruptcy.

As has been mentioned, the greatest problem facing the farmers is that of the overpopulation. Despite the expenditure of tremendous amounts of man-power and capital since the end of the war to open up new land for farming, the total amount of cultivated land remains much the same. This is because increases in acreage have been canceled out by the appropriation of farmland for factories and houses. Land has also been lost as the result of natural dis-asters. There is still hope for developing farmland in mountainous regions and on the island of Hokkaido, but though any additional acreage will be welcome, it cannot solve the overpopulation. The agricultural population (including fishing and forestry) continues to grow, despite migration to the cities, and this increasing number of people is receiving a steadily decreasing share of the national income. In 1957 agricultural workers, some forty per cent of the working force, contributed only 13.5 per cent of the total income. It seems obvious that palliatives like the proposed reclamation projects cannot by themselves supply a solution, though they may relieve some of the acute pressure.

Meanwhile the farmers, for all the labor-saving devices which recent years have brought some of them, lead much the lives of their ancestors. The chief crop almost everywhere is rice, a plant which requires long hours of tedious and disagree-able work. The men and women in the rice paddies, wading up to their knees (or deeper) in the mud, replanting in the traditional manner the delicate shoots, cannot hope that in the near future mechanical inventions will lighten their tasks.

They are free, however, from one heartache known to farmers elsewhere: there is no danger that oversupply will keep them from selling their rice at decent prices. Not enough rice is grown in Japan to meet domestic needs, and large quantities must be imported from Southeast Asia and the United States. The Japanese do not relish "foreign rice," and whatever is grown at home is sure to find a market.

The government has attempted with varying success to persuade the Japa-nese people to modify their diet. Full milling of rice removes three quarters of vitamin B_1, the lack of which may bring on beriberi and digestive com-plaints. In time of dire shortages the government has been able to enforce the consumption of half-milled rice or of rice served with an admixture of wheat, but as soon as rice becomes more plentiful people insist on eating white rice.

Rice is definitely a staple food for the Japanese in a way that neither bread

83 An old carpenter uses a long, old-fashioned saw which makes it easier to cut straight.

84 A carpenter takes the first step in building a house: a rough framework of bamboo poles tied together with ropes.

85–86 Skilled craftsmen like these potters turn out traditional wares in their own shops.

83

84

85

86

87   HIDEO HAGA: CHUOKORON-SHA

88

WERNER BISCHOF: MAGNUM

nor potatoes is for Europeans. The other dishes served at a meal are supplemental, flavorings which help down the bowls of rice. The British sociologist R.P. Dore has aptly said, "A proper appreciation of rice (involving necessarily a horror for foreign rice) is valued as highly in a Japanese as a discriminating palate for wines in an upper-class Englishman." Foreign writers sometimes mention with dismay the fact that for many Japanese a handful of rice and some dried fish make a meal, but their sympathy may be misplaced: the Emperor himself probably eats a similar diet much of the time. Almost everybody in Japan is content with rice and considers himself well-fed if he can get his fill of the Japanese variety.

The demand for rice naturally exerts an enormous influence on Japanese agriculture. It means, for example, that parts of the country whose climate is essentially unsuited to rice-growing must be given over to this purpose. Attempts to open new land are also hampered by the fact that unless it can produce rice, exploitation is unlikely to be profitable. The Japanese diet has changed since the Meiji Restoration, but it has largely been in the direction of a general consumption of rice and fish (formerly the privilege of the rich) rather than of foreign foods.

Meat-eating had always been prohibited by Buddhist law before the Meiji Restoration. Fowl were consumed on special occasions, and rabbits were classified as birds so that people might eat them with clear consciences, but the meat of four-footed animals was traditionally considered repugnant. Even today some old Japanese become nauseous if beef or pork is served in the same room where they are eating. However, the passion for Westernization led many enlightened men to advocate beef-eating as a means of improving the Japanese physique and intelligence. Abattoirs were opened in the 1860's for the benefit of foreign residents, and before long "beef-shops" were springing up in Tokyo and serving *sukiyaki* to Japanese as an enlightened Western dish. It looked as though Japan were going to abandon her traditional preference for fish in favor of the new delicacy, but this never happened. Meat remains to this day a luxury, and even those who can afford it generally like fish better.

FISHING

Fishing in Japan is of two kinds: the daily work of men manning their own boats, and the large-scale operations of companies which own whole fleets of fishing craft. The latter have developed into a modern industry with far-flung activities. Floating crab-canneries roam the north Pacific, and other fleets go far into the south Pacific for tuna. Fishery treaties are always of vital concern to the Japanese, and atomic bomb explosions are likely to endanger the lives of Japanese fishermen, no matter how remote the corner of the Pacific.

87 In some remote districts women still spin cloth by hand, usually for the benefit of city patrons of arts and crafts.

88 The dyed silk is dried in the wind.

133

The traditional fishing, based on small ports scattered along the entire coasts, represents a distinctive part of Japanese life. Fishing is an even riskier occupation than farming, for a fisherman often returns home exhausted with a scanty or unsaleable catch. Unlike the farmers (fifty per cent of whom eat the rice they grow) the fishermen usually sell all marketable fish, and content themselves with tasteless varieties or with clams and squid. In many villages along the Japan Sea coast, for example, squid is the most common item in the diet. Some fishermen also cultivate fields—or rather, their wives do, while the men are at sea. Their life is a dreary one relieved by few entertainments, and though the fishermen today may enjoy electricity and a few other modern conveniences in their villages, they are usually poorer and more backward than the farmers. The fishing communities are the last stronghold of some of the superstitions of the past which the rest of Japan is so anxious to disown.

89   Silks dyed in Kyoto are washed in the clear rivers. When the rivers flow red or purple, the people know that times are prosperous.

INDUSTRY SINCE THE WAR

By the time that the war ended in 1945 many of Japan's factories were shattered by the bombings and others contained nothing more than rusting machinery under broken roofs. The Allied Occupation forces, anxious to destroy Japan's war potential, proposed that a large proportion of the factories which had survived the war be dismantled and sent abroad to satisfy claims for war reparations against Japan. During the black days of 1945 and 1946, when most Japanese had hardly enough to eat, such proposals must have sounded like the knell of doom; any further reduction of Japan's productive capacity would have made a recovery all the less probable. But the policy of dismantling factories was never, in fact, carried out. The Occupation authorities found it expedient instead to save the Japanese economy, and to this end they encouraged a revival of productive capacity.

No one could have foreseen the recovery which actually took place, an amazing one even for the industrious Japanese. Less than ten years after 1945, when the Japanese surveyed with despair their crippled industrial plants, they were proudly saying that the "post-war was over," meaning that output had gone far beyond the point of a mere recovery. In 1957 the index of industrial production stood at 277.3 as compared to a norm of 100 for 1934–1936. Recovery has been especially notable in heavy industry. Japanese-built ships now sail under many flags, and steel, industrial plants and machinery rank as leading exports.

90   Unlike most cities crisscrossed by rivers, Kyoto keeps its waterways very clean.

Low prices ceased to be the sole selling point of Japanese goods. Even items costing more than the prevailing world prices managed to find markets because of their quality or the speed of delivery. Before the war textiles (mainly raw silk) formed over half the Japanese exports, and though still important

89

90

91

TOGE FUJIHIRA

92

93

during the post-war recovery, they were part of a much more diversified list of exports. The textiles now sold were mainly cottons and synthetic fabrics, including some invented by the Japanese. It remained as necessary as ever to import the raw materials which Japan lacks—cotton, wool, petroleum, sugar, etc.—but the Japanese showed themselves increasingly able to do without large imports of manufactured products.

The ability demonstrated by the Japanese to manufacture the most advanced products of modern industry has come mainly from their amazing achievements in the sciences during the past half-century. Lafcadio Hearn, writing in 1895, declared, "However widely diffused among the people, scientific education cannot immediately raise the average of practical intelligence to the Western level. The common capacity must remain low for generations." But at present Japanese traveling in foreign countries frequently comment on how much poorer at arithmetic shop clerks are than those in Japan, and the "common capacity" has risen very rapidly. On the highest levels, Japan has produced a Nobel Prize winner in physics, Dr. Hideki Yukawa, and in all the sciences Japanese are prominent.

Another source of Japanese skill in making lenses, precision instruments and so on may be the heritage from traditional crafts. The men who today make transistor radios have the dexterity of the craftsmen who carved sword ornaments a hundred years ago. Traditional crafts have not been entirely displaced today by modern industry. Even while high-speed machines are busily grinding out millions of yards of synthetic cloth at factories all over Japan, fine silks are being woven by hand, some by a technique of fingernail embroidery known to hardly a dozen men. Modern techniques have made possible some advances in sericulture, but the silk industry is inevitably based on the worm and the mulberry leaf and all the time-consuming steps to the final product. Traditional skills are prized as ever, whether in weaving, textile design or dyeing. The famous *yuzen* process by which complicated floral and bird patterns are transferred to silk through repeated dyeings is still carried on in Kyoto.

Many old crafts rank as arts. Lacquer, bamboo-work and hand-made paper have captured the fancy of shoppers abroad by their charm and beauty. Before the war the Japanese tended to export only objects in what they considered to be the foreign tastes, meaning that they were garish if not downright hideous. They have not given up this trade in souvenirs and baubles: the quaint little English toby jugs, the Dresden china shepherdesses, the Indian squaws with papooses and the rest of the inexpensive objects which clutter our gift shops often as not bear the name "Japan." The amount of money realized from such imitations undoubtedly exceeds by many times the sales of beautiful genuinely Japanese wares. Nevertheless, more reputable products of the native artistic genius are now also earning foreign exchange.

Before the war the chief markets for Japanese goods were China, Korea,

91   *At Yawata, one of the largest steel mills in the world rises above traditional gray-tiled roofs.*

92   *A young construction worker studies blueprints. Many Japanese cities were leveled during the war by bombings, but have since been entirely rebuilt.*

93   *In such yards Japan today builds more ships than any other country in the world.*

and other areas of Eastern Asia under Japanese domination. Political developments since the war have denied these markets to Japan.

Japan's largest market is now the United States, which in 1957 bought over 20 per cent of Japan's exports, mainly textiles and other inexpensive products of medium and small industries. The second largest market, oddly enough, was Liberia. Ships accounted for 99.6 per cent of the exports to Liberia, a country whose laws make it convenient for Greek shipowners to register their vessels there. Other important markets are in Southeast Asia and South America, but unlike the pre-war pattern, Japanese exports and markets are today quite diversified. In 1936, for example, 35 per cent of the exports went to China and Korea, and 56 per cent of the exports were textiles. Today no country (with the exception of the United States) buys more than 5 per cent of Japan's exports, and metal products, chemicals and machinery rank nearly as high as textiles on the export list. Trade with China and the Soviet Union, long a subject of lively controversy, has as yet not assumed major proportions.

The Japanese must export in order to pay for foodstuffs and necessary raw materials. However, the increasing cost of Japanese goods has made it harder for the Japanese to win customers in competitive markets. One of the factors is the improvement in the standard of living of Japanese workers, due largely to the unions.

Before the war unions were weak, and it was possible for manufacturers to keep labor costs low by housing workers in dormitories and paying minimal wages. The American Occupation authorities, deploring such practices, encouraged the growth of unions. Their membership in 1958 reached over 6,500,000, of whom one quarter were women. Organized labor has been effective in promoting the demands of workers for higher wages and better conditions. This has naturally increased labor costs in organized industries. Moreover, even though the wages of the individual worker may be much lower than in the United States or Europe, more workers are usually needed to turn out a given product, and total labor costs may actually be higher. Automation and other labor-saving systems are being tried experimentally, but in an overpopulated country any steps to reduce the number of jobs is almost unthinkable, however desirable in terms of making Japanese goods cheaper.

The leaders in foreign trade are much the same companies today as before the war. Mitsui, Mitsubishi and the rest have re-emerged under their old names after a period when they ostensibly complied with Occupation orders to dissolve into small independent firms. These huge companies engage in an astonishing variety of activities, and Japanese economists see a steady tendency for them to monopolize the major manufacturing industries. As the big companies grow stronger, the little businessman is harder pressed to survive, and many now think of economic improvement in terms of political change.

94-95 Such Japanese products as automobiles, cameras and watches are now often welcomed in other countries, not, as they once were, because of price but because of quality.

96 In contests between an abacus and an adding machine, the abacus usually wins. No Japanese office is without them.

97 Japanese typewriters have about 2,000 keys to cope with the thousands of characters used in writing Japanese.

94   MARC RIBOUD: MAGNUM

95   JAPANESE CONSULATE GENERAL, NEW YORK

96   JAPANESE CONSULATE GENERAL, NEW YORK

JAPANESE CONSULATE GENERAL, NEW YORK

97

98

99

Chapter VII

DEMOCRACY IN AN EASTERN TRADITION

THE IMPERIAL FAMILY

*98 The Emperor and Empress
with their grandchildren at home.
The Emperor's residence was
moved from Kyoto to Tokyo
in 1869.*

*99 The Crown Prince and his
Princess met on the tennis courts, a
suitably modern beginning for a
romance that upset a thousand-
year-old tradition.*

AS RECENTLY AS 1945 the Japanese "national polity" was based on the belief that Japan was utterly unlike all other countries, a unique family-nation benevolently guided by a divine ruler. The Emperor, a descendant of the Sun Goddess through a line of "ten thousand generations," was the focal point of the patriotism and devotion of all Japanese. Today Japan is a constitutional monarchy with a government very similar to that of democratic European monarchies. The Emperor, according to the post-war constitution, "derives his position from the will of the people with whom resides sovereign power." His functions are largely symbolic—receiving ambassadors and opening the Japanese parliament—and the people, through their elected delegates, now rule over the Land of the Gods.

The outward manifestations of emperor-worship, so common a couple of decades ago, have all but vanished today. The Emperor divested himself of his divinity by a proclamation, and his subjects have since been encouraged to think of him with affection rather than with awe and trembling. The "emperor-system" is openly and loudly attacked. Newspapers which not so long ago faced immediate suspension for the faintest suggestion of disrespect, now print articles and cartoons making light of the sacred monarchical institutions. Nevertheless the office of Emperor with its traditions remains today the most distinctive feature of the Japanese government.

The present Emperor is the 124th of his line according to the traditional accounts, which further date the "coronation" of his distant ancestor Jimmu, the founder of the nation, in 660 B.C. Modern scholars, however, believe that even if the total number of rulers is approximately correct, the dynasty is not older than the Christian era. Japan first appears in recorded history at the end of the third century A.D., when a Chinese historian described the visit of one of his compatriots to the land of the "eastern barbarians." At that time, he informs us, the Japanese were a simple but amiable people living in over a hundred communities ruled over by a queen.

The earliest surviving Japanese book, the *Record of Ancient Matters,* was presented to the court in 712 A.D. and is a glorification of the lineage and achievements of the Imperial Family. Even in the old histories, however, the distinction was made between the august, unspeakable majesty of the office of emperor, and the sometimes less than admirable qualities of the actual men. The sixth-century Emperor Buretsu, for example, is reported to have ordered innocent men to climb trees in order that he might have the pleasure of shooting them down with his arrows; and in the following centuries we read numerous instances of emperors murdered by their successors or murderously inclined themselves, of simpletons, dipsomaniacs, bigots and debauchees—as well as some thoroughly admirable rulers. These facts were admitted by Japanese scholars even during periods when ultranationalism colored scholarship; the emperors, though divine, were allowed human failings.

Despite its aura of majesty the Imperial Family has enjoyed only relatively brief periods of prosperity during the past thousand years. Most of this time the ruling power was in other hands—the prime minister's, a retired emperor's, or a general's. It is astonishing that the imperial line survived these vicissitudes.

The imperial fortunes sank to their lowest ebb in the sixteenth century, when the body of one emperor could not be buried for lack of funeral money, and another emperor supported himself by making souvenirs and selling specimens of his handwriting. Yet before the same century was over, the emperor's finances improved remarkably thanks to the unexpected generosity of the real rulers, who were soldiers.

In the eighteenth century studies of the ancient Japanese classics began to attract important scholars, and research which had been purely philological developed into ultranationalistic speculation. The perusal of such works as the *Record of Ancient Matters* convinced these scholars of the mystic and sacred character of the Imperial House.

However, even the scholars who spoke with such reverence and rapture of the Imperial Family were probably ignorant of (and uninterested in) the person who was actually occupying the throne. The emperor's activities were confined to a few ritual duties, and his subjects saw nothing of him. Graceful compliments and allusions were sometimes made to the shogun in the literature of the time, but the emperor remained (in the old phrase) "above the clouds." Not surprisingly, it was only in the nineteenth century that foreign countries dealing with Japan suspected the existence of a higher authority than the shogun. The Chinese, for example, had been accustomed for centuries to address letters to the shogun with the title "King of Japan." The emperors for their part were either too young or too cautious to assert themselves; two emperors who tried to exercise the power nominally theirs had been driven into exile by the real masters of Japan.

The emperor had thus been a ceremonial figurehead by long tradition when the Restoration of 1868 brought to the youthful Emperor Meiji a considerable measure of authority. The capital was moved from Kyoto to the shogunate capital of Edo (which was then given the name of Tokyo, or Eastern Capital), in order to dramatize the Emperor's assumption of the political power of the shogun. The new Emperor and his advisers, though they worked always for the modernization of Japan, deliberately fostered the ideals of the mysterious "national polity" which made the Emperor divine. Meiji, however, was more than a symbol; fortunately for the Japanese, he was a gifted and conscientious ruler, and he deserved the admiration as well as the respect of his people.

The Emperor Meiji was by no means the sole authority in the new Japan. Some of the men surrounding him used the cry "Respect the Emperor!" as a convenient way to arouse public enthusiasm for their own projects. Some rallying symbol for the people was necessary. Had the Meiji Restoration been a different kind of revolution, the leaders might have declared its aims to be life, liberty and the pursuit of happiness, but, realizing that their nation lacked the traditions implied by such slogans, they justified their revolution in terms of a restoration of imperial power. It might have been hard to persuade the mass of the people to exert themselves for the sake of modernization had there been no emperor, at once a god and a father concerned for his children, exhorting them.

When the Emperor Meiji succeeded to the throne, Japan was an obscure monarchy centuries behind Europe, but before he died Japan had defeated Russia and won an equal alliance with England. This spectacular success cost the Japanese people many hardships, and the policies of the government were often undemocratic, foreshadowing the later abuses of emperor-worship, but the magnificent achievement of the Restoration cannot be disputed. Today the Emperor Meiji is revered as the bringer of "enlightened rule"—the literal meaning of the name Meiji.

Meiji's successor, the Emperor Taishô, never captured his people's imagination in the manner his father had, partly because of his own personality, partly because the changes which Japan underwent during his reign were less exhilarating to the nation.

Taishô's son, the present Emperor, became regent in 1921 because of his father's illness, and he succeeded to the throne in 1926. As Crown Prince he had traveled to Europe, much to the consternation of some of his advisers, who feared unfortunate consequences from an exposure to Western institutions. Their fears were not without foundation: the story is told that one day after the Crown Prince's return to Tokyo he expressed a wish to take a stroll downtown, as he had often done in London and Paris. None of his advisers answered the prince, but instead each rose, and respectfully bowing, quietly left the room. The prince, left alone in the darkening, empty room, could only shout in fury at his own helplessness.

This anecdote typifies his relations as Emperor with the military leaders who ruled Japan in the 1930's and 1940's. Ultranationalistic movements which threatened to destroy parliamentary government constantly invoked his name, and assassinations were justified as acts freeing the Emperor of evil counselors. Yet all this was done without reference to the real desires of the Emperor. On one occasion, at least, the Emperor expressed himself openly on the subject of revolutionary nationalism by ordering rebellious soldiers back to their barracks. Nevertheless, the fiery nationalists went on disregarding the Emperor in the name of the Emperor, or rather in the name of the position. The Emperor himself, a quiet, scholarly man devoted to marine biology, was ignored. Tens of thousands of Japanese soldiers died under the impression that they were obeying the Emperor's wishes, though he disliked war.

Few of his subjects suspected how distressed he was by the activities of the militarists, and he sought no contact with the people. When he visited a school or a hospital everyone had to keep his head bowed during the entire visit, and it was even forbidden for students to lift their eyes to his photograph when it was unveiled in their school on ceremonial occasions. He (or at any rate his position) was worshipped, but by becoming a god he had lost the claim on human affection. The most colorless European ruler inspired more love than this man for whose sake millions were prepared unhesitatingly to throw away their lives. When, in August 1945, he read on the radio the proclamation ending the war, his voice was totally unfamiliar and the language remote, and despite his explicit command that the fighting stop, some patriotic soldiers attempted to continue the war, still in his name.

The Emperor could have had no idea what the Americans had in store for him. Indeed, he had every reason to suppose that he would be tried as a war criminal. On the occasion of his first meeting with General MacArthur he is reported to have announced his willingness to take on himself the guilt of the entire nation. The Occupation authorities, however, decided that it would be wiser to leave him as the head of a nominally independent state, rather than risk insubordination from the people, and no charges were ever brought against him.

On January 1, 1946 the Emperor issued his celebrated proclamation in which he stated that he was not divine, and that the Japanese people were not superior to other races of the world. He expressed the belief also that the ties between himself and his people were of trust and affection, and not dependent on the old legends and myths. His statement was accepted with astounding equanimity by the Japanese. Photographs of the Imperial Family which had been displayed in every house were quietly removed, and the same teacher who months earlier would have risked death in the flames to save the Emperor's picture if the school had been burning, now turned the worship hall into an extra classroom.

To prove the mutual bonds of affection between the Emperor and his subjects, he was expected to mingle affably with crowds, and, as a democratic monarch, to inquire politely about damage suffered in the war or prospects for reconstruction. Some pathetic newsreels taken at the time show the Emperor uncertainly bobbing and bowing through crowds which a short time before could not have looked on his face without fear of a policeman's saber. The Emperor continued in the following years to make personal appearances all over the country, but he did not seem happy in the role, and "democratic" visits became infrequent. Though no longer a god, in the eyes of his subjects he is still not completely human. Despite the published photographs of the Imperial Family relaxing amidst the bourgeois Western furnishings of the palace, one cannot imagine the Emperor chatting with his subjects, or even with the most distinguished men of the realm. He is most successful still in his symbolic functions, when he appears a tiny, distant figure before the hundreds of thousands of people milling outside the palace at New Year.

Warmer feelings are entertained towards the Empress and especially the Crown Prince. The Empress has the plump, motherly lines favored in queens everywhere, and it is easy to believe from her photographs that she is a devoted wife and mother.

Most of the Japanese enthusiasm for the Imperial Family is concentrated in the person of the Crown Prince. His picture (though not his parents') graces the alcoves of innumerable houses, particularly in the country, and he shares albums of photographs and the walls of barber shops with the reigning movie stars. Japanese parents sometimes complain that under the new educational system their children know nothing about the Emperor and cannot even recognize his photograph, but every school child is familiar with the activities of the Crown Prince. When he returned from abroad in 1953 after attending the coronation of Queen Elizabeth II, millions of school children enthusiastically welcomed him back. The Crown Prince became the subject of a best-selling novel, *The Lonely One,* written by a high-school classmate, and incidents related in the novel of the prince's sporadic and feeble attempts to be "just another boy" caught the public imagination. Many people came to feel that the prince stood for the new Japan, and was not merely an upholder of old traditions. His decision to marry a commoner, greeted with immense excitement, confirmed this view. Even opponents of the monarchy, for all their wry comments, were moved by this dramatic gesture.

Most Japanese today undoubtedly favor the retention of the Emperor, though few could offer reasons why. Little personal attachment is involved—it would still be thought somehow sacrilegious to say that he was "good" either as a man or emperor. Instead, there is an imprecise feeling along the lines of, "We've always had an emperor, so I suppose we ought to keep having one." Better educated people may mention the emperor's historical significance or his value as a symbol of the Japanese people, but for many more Japanese he is still the personification of authority.

POLITICS AND THE WAR

The first session of the Diet was held in 1890, the year following the proclamation of the Meiji Constitution. Political parties, however, had been organized as far back as the 1870's, and lively activity on their part had preceded parliamentary debate. Some students of Japanese politics have made much of the fact that neither the Meiji Constitution nor the later one of 1947 (dictated by the Allied Occupation forces) came into being as the result of the struggles of the common people, as was the case in many other countries. However, not all nations have advanced towards democracy by identical methods, and though both Japanese constitutions were bestowed from above, they closely accorded with popular desires. The position of the Emperor, for example, was defined in both constitutions in terms which accurately reflected prevailing opinion. Even the reforms instituted by the Americans after the war were in the direction which the Japanese themselves would have taken if left to their own tendencies.

100 A politician addresses a May Day rally. His speech includes such exhortations as "Unify our struggle," "Crush militarism," and "Overthrow the Cabinet!".

This does not mean that government in Japan has always followed the wishes of the people. Far from it. During the half-century prior to the outbreak of war in 1941, the men of state repeatedly allowed themselves to be overawed and even dominated by the military. Both "China Incidents" of the 1930's, for example, were initiated by the army without the consent or even the knowledge of the representatives of the people. The militarists were able to have their way because the cabinet had to include Army and Navy officers, and if they refused to participate, a cabinet could not be formed. Even the Emperor was helpless to control the right-wing fanatics.

The lack of protection against the military was the fatal flaw in the Meiji Constitution. Their triumph in the 1930's and 1940's is an ugly fact of Japanese history which cannot be ignored, no matter how favorably disposed towards Japan one may be. This revolutionary nationalism was essentially an irrational movement, which denied economic and political realities in the name of a mystic purification of the nation. The young officers who headed the movement bitterly attacked what they termed the "corruption and degeneracy" of the political parties, and of the statesmen and generals in power.

101 Women have had the right to vote in Japan only since the end of the war. Here a country woman, carrying a child, registers.

100

ROBERT CAPA: MAGNUM

101

HORACE BRISTOL

102   TERUAKI TOMATSU: CHUOKORON-SHA

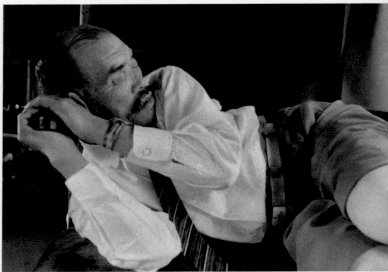

103   TERUAKI TOMATSU: CHUOKORON-SHA

104   TERUAKI TOMATSU: CHUOKORON-SHA

TERUAKI TOMATSU: CHUOKORON-SHA

105

Their denunciations of capitalists as men who oppress the agrarian and laboring classes hardly differed in expression from those of the Communists, but the regeneration of Japan they proposed was in the name of the Emperor. Little constructive planning accompanied these attacks. The object of the assassinations which they provoked could only have been a military dictatorship which was hardly likely to improve conditions. Several prime ministers and other public figures fell victims to such conspiracies.

What strikes us most forcefully about the assassins is that they were not moved by personal ambition. They obviously desired to act in a just and noble manner, regardless of the sacrifices which might be entailed. Most of them expected death, and even those who were successful did not benefit in any material way from their deeds. Unlike the Nazis, for example, they remained poor—a fact which surprised American investigators after the war. The young officers and the various military cliques were duped by their own ideals. They ruined the country they loved and led to death millions whom they had sworn to help. They themselves fought with incredible bravery. Their simple-minded devotion was worthy of a better cause.

The war precipitated by Japanese attacks on Pearl Harbor demanded steadily greater sacrifices from the whole nation. A year of victories was followed by three of defeats. Tens of thousands of soldiers vanished in the jungles of the South Seas. Japan's own cities were ravaged by bombings, and the people were weak with exhaustion and hunger. Yet there was no suggestion of revolt, and even complaints were few. Japanese in later years recall the war with loathing, but look back on it also as a time when extraordinary unselfishness was common. The unspeakable horror of the atomic bombs called forth acts of magnificent heroism and generosity.

Hardly had the war ended than the Japanese were informed that all they had believed for years to be just and good was wrong. With a wholehearted devotion that astonished the world, they immediately switched to principles which had been anathema to them. Innumerable foreign observers have since opined (often on the basis of a very slight acquaintance with the country) that changes in Japan have only been on the surface. It will take years before we can tell whether or not these judgments are correct, but certainly much has been permanently affected. At first, of course, a natural reaction to the policies of the militarists, which had brought so much suffering, led to pro-democratic manifestations. Again, when the Japanese discovered that the Americans, contrary to what their own propaganda had led them to believe, were not monsters, many swung easily to the other extreme and admired everything American. The high ideals of the Greater East Asia War were sloughed off with surprising ease. "Pure Japanese" words invented during the war for foreign importations like ice cream, shovel and bus were replaced by the old familiar words *aisukurimu*, *shaberu* and *basu*. The Japanese tried to salvage what was left

---

Caption (left margin):

102 *Politics at the grass roots: a local leader, member of a prefectural assembly, enjoys a laugh with some of his constituents.*

103 *Train journeys around his constituency give him a chance to nap.*

104 *Home in his own town, he catches up on local news with his eldest son. Most farmers vote conservative.*

105 *He also keeps in touch with the district by traveling on foot. Such country "bosses" usually control the vote in their districts.*

of their pre-militaristic traditions, and eagerly adopted many of the most obvious and unattractive features of American culture.

Not all Japanese, of course, were so easily converted to the new ideals. Even today ultranationalists survive in small numbers, often recognizable by their closely-cropped hair, mustaches and muscular physiques. Some periodicals cater to their preferences, and meetings, addressed chiefly by men prominent during the war, draw them forth from their obscurity. Young bravos, nostalgic for a militarism they themselves never experienced, also attend such meetings, as do old gentlemen who still mention the Imperial Family only with trepidation. The right wing is still capable of staging occasional demonstrations, but it would be hard to find evidence for the charge that the old militarism still lurks beneath the surface of the new Japan.

For the most part the Japanese were thoroughly disgusted with the war by the time it concluded, and they are sincere in their protestations against rearmament. Even the soldiers of the present Self-Defence Force feel uncomfortable in uniforms when off duty, and seem rather ashamed of their profession. When foreign observers point out to a Japanese that an adequate defence force is essential to Japanese security, the answer is often that surrender to invaders would be preferable to another war.

POLITICS TODAY

Politics in Japan today is the object of the liveliest attention throughout the country. Since the war the Japanese have enjoyed universal suffrage, and a great range of political viewpoints is represented in the Diet. The Diet (parliament) in Tokyo consists of two chambers—a House of Councilors and a House of Representatives. The former is the successor of the House of Peers provided for under the Meiji Constitution, and a result of the abolition of the peerage. It is a deliberative body elected for six-year terms. Representatives serve four-year terms unless the premier dissolves the body for an election. Each of the prefectures also has a legislative body, and the cities and towns have councils.

The biggest party is the Liberal-Democratic, a conservative coalition which draws its strength mainly from the farmers, the businessmen, and the older people in general. Frequent disputes among its would-be leaders reflect their political convictions less than their personalities and ambitions. Any politician who believes that he has a chance of becoming prime minister is tempted to overthrow the existing cabinet even though he may agree essentially with its policies.

Division among the Socialists (the second political party), on the other hand, is based on deeper issues. Formerly they were split into two distinct groups. The right-wing Socialists resembled the Labour Party of Great Britain, but the left-wing Socialists were often in agreement with the Communists. The united Socialist Party is backed by the unions, the intellectuals, and most young people. Its failure to excite greater support among the farmers may be the result of the Socialists' preference for basing campaigns on abstract issues rather than on immediate needs such as new roads or housing. Too often they have denounced the conservatives without offering suggestions of their own, and therefore some people fear that if the Socialists assumed power there would be a period of confusion and inefficiency. On the other hand, it may be argued that once the Socialists are given greater opportunities to familiarize themselves with practical administration problems, they will quickly become more astute and constructive.

The Communists and allied parties control only a few seats in the Diet, but their actual strength is undoubtedly much more impressive. Their organization has also been torn by dissension, partly occasioned by criticism from Moscow. Up until 1950 the Japanese Communist Party's policy was to be "lovable," but its methods were abruptly changed in that year (seemingly in connection with the Korean War) to those of an aggressively revolutionary party. This line has since been abandoned, but memories of the Communists' violence at that time left a bad taste in the mouths of Japanese. The only candidates for the Diet whom the Communists regularly succeed in electing are those who were thrown into prison during the war, or were forced to become refugees abroad; i.e., men whose fame attracts more votes than their platforms.

It seems likely that the conservatives will remain in power for the time being. The Socialist Party has grown in strength, even in the rural areas, but the conservatives maintain their predominance, if only because most small towns vote as the local boss dictates, and he is usually conservative. It is true that the ballot is secret, but the small-town "boss," who knows all his constituents intimately, can usually tell who has swerved from his orders. In one famous instance, when a conservative "boss" was succeeded by his radical son, the village abruptly switched from voting unanimously for the conservative party to a unanimous Communist vote! In recent years parent-teacher groups and other village organizations have weened some voters away from their traditional boss-dictated balloting, but bosses still retain their authority, often because they are, in fact, the most capable men in the village. The boss is in a position to do favors for his constituents, and he does not let them forget it. A new bridge, the result of the boss's lobbying in the Diet, is a more powerful inducement to vote conservative than the vague, general promises of improvement offered by the Socialists.

Most unions support left-wing Socialist or Communist candidates, but not all union members vote as their leaders suggest. Some members of the violently progressive teachers' union, for example, are conservative, and many others are completely uninterested in politics. Nevertheless, the funds of the union are made available to the Socialists and not to the conservatives, and the leaders speak for the entire union in their political pronouncements.

Intellectuals also tend to be leftist. Communism as such does not necessarily attract them, but Marxism does, and even those who dislike Communism are unlikely to become anti-Communist, if only because they remember how the wartime government immediately labeled anyone it disliked a "Communist." Events at home and abroad are constantly shifting the allegiances of the intellectuals. The anti-Stalin speeches in the U.S.S.R., for example, shook many left-wing students, and the Hungarian rebellion disillusioned still others. There has been a general thawing of the solid anti-American front of the early 1950's, though many who are quick to attack the United States on the flimsiest of evidence still hesitate to express opinions unfavorable to the U.S.S.R. because, they say, they "lack sufficient information." The "new China" has exerted an even greater appeal than the U.S.S.R. on Japanese intellectuals, and the process of disillusion has been slower. Intellectuals, even those chiefly concerned with fine arts or the theater, frequently expound their political views, which are sought by the newspapers, especially just before an election.

Election campaigns in Japan are lively and noisy. Three to five members of the House of Representatives are chosen in each election district from about twice that number of candidates. Posters showing the candidates' photographs are plastered on walls throughout the town, and the candidates themselves make numerous appearances, often speaking from open trucks. Loudspeakers mounted on these trucks blast out the candidate's name over and over in hypnotizing rhythms. New election regulations require the candidates to make speeches in between repetitions of their name, but some of them get around this by inserting only meaningless phrases: "Tanaka Kazuo stands for... Tanaka Kazuo is your candidate..." At election meetings, whether of one party or of all candidates, more cogent statements of platforms are expected.

A typical city election meeting is held in the evening in a school gymnasium. If it is winter the room will be barely heated, and the crowd huddles together around old-fashioned stoves. The candidates know in advance which platforms will please a particular audience, and they are likely to modify their views to suit the occasion. A conservative candidate speaking in a district known to be unfriendly to rearmament will either omit all mention of the subject or else express his opposition to it, though he knows that if elected he will be obliged to follow his party in voting to amend the constitution so as to permit rearmament. Similarly, a Socialist candidate speaking in a conservative district will emphasize the fact that he is not a Communist, and will stress his allegiance to parliamentary institutions; in a left-wing district he will not go out of his way to alienate possible Communist support.

Some speakers favor the florid style of oratory popular in Japan ever since the Meiji Restoration, piling mellifluous but often meaningless adjectives on their familiar phrases. The Liberal-Democratic candidate may voice his concern over the problems of youth or propose homes for the aged like those he has seen in America. The Socialist will point out in anguished tones the plight of small business and the underpaid workers. The Communist, with a wave of the sheaf of papers he holds in his hands, "proves" that two thirds of the Japanese national income is being siphoned off into American pockets, and insists that Japan is no more than an American dependency. If an ultranationalist is standing for office, the candidate of the Japanese Production Party or the Anti-Bolshevization League, he will describe the terrible menace of the U.S.S.R. and declare that the Socialists no less than the Communists are under orders from Moscow. He will then go on to imply that the conservatives are under orders from Washington. Both the United States and the U.S.S.R. arouse equal distaste in him, and he shouts excitedly, "When I look on the lamentable, cruel, tragic state of Japan today, I ask myself what is to be done. We must build a warm, loving, sympathetic government which will rescue Japan from its present utter and abject misery."

The audience listens attentively, enjoying the oratory. Sometimes voices shout approval, but more often the comments are sardonic. When the speaker announces that he is the candidate of the Liberal-Democratic Party, he may, for example, be greeted with a cry of "The party of corruption!" The heckled speaker usually ignores the outburst, but he may heatedly deny the charge— "No, Socialists are not Communists!" "No, the Japanese Production Party is not run by hoodlums!" The impression produced by a candidate at such a meeting weighs with some voters, but many others are influenced by seemingly extraneous factors—feelings of sympathy for the runner-up in the previous election, or attachment for a representative of long standing. This is why men who are strongly suspected of corruption, or who are known to have been disorderly in the Diet, may nevertheless be elected.

Election results are prominently displayed around the town—in front of the railway station, in bank and shop windows, outside municipal buildings. The five winning candidates are likely to cover the political spectrum, from the conservative old lawyer to the youngish union leader. A popular orator, an old Socialist and an earnest housewife may complete the list. In some country districts, however, all winning candidates may be of the same land-owning, conservative type.

Japanese elections (like those in many countries) have their seamy side—deals behind the scenes, candidates who win office by immense expenditures, last-minute shifts of votes. But the elections are free and reflect the wishes of the voters.

It is hard to say how deeply democracy is rooted among the Japanese, and whether they would fight for the privilege of choosing their government. The Japanese would probably not battle in the streets to protect the vote, but they certainly appreciate its importance, and any attempt to impose tyranny now would arouse greater opposition than ever before. The record of the Japanese Diet, even in recent years, has not always been impressive. Its sessions have been marred particularly by physical violence. Nevertheless the failure of democracy in many other Asian countries makes us appreciate Japan's success in establishing a stable, representative government. More than anything else Japanese democracy needs time to establish itself, not merely as what their leaders consider to be the "proper" thing to believe in, but as an inalienable right of all Japanese.

Chapter VIII

EDUCATION:

A GREAT DEBATE

THE OLD STYLE

FORMAL EDUCATION in Japan began only after the introduction of Chinese writing in the sixth century A.D. Even before that time some people—priests and poets—were no doubt instructed in the sacred legends of the gods and heroes, but there was nothing resembling a school. By the eighth century, however, education had progressed so far that an ability to write Chinese was indispensable in a courtier, and a university was founded to train sons of the nobility in the Confucian classics. The courtiers eagerly studied and imitated not only the philosophical texts but Chinese literature. The education of court ladies, on the other hand, was usually confined to Japanese poetry. Lady Murasaki, author of *The Tale of Genji,* described in her diary how she managed to learn the Chinese classics only by eavesdropping on her brother's lessons. The most conspicuous sign of a good education for either a man or woman was fine penmanship and the ability to recognize poetic allusions.

So genteel an education was, needless to say, for the leisure classes only. The government had no intention of educating the populace, "it being an accepted principle," as G.B. Sansom points out in *The Western World and Japan,* "that the people must be made to obey and not to learn." The common people learned more through the ears than the eyes. Sermons, parables and the tales of storytellers continued to be important sources of knowledge for them at least until the seventeenth century, when peace and greater prosperity for the merchant class gave commoners a much better chance to obtain an education. Schools sprang up all over Japan. At first the teachers were mainly Buddhist priests—the transmitters of Japanese culture during the dark period of the civil wars—and their schools were known as *terakoya,* or "temple schools."

The typical *terakoya* of the seventeenth or eighteenth century was a one-roomed schoolhouse presided over by a single teacher and attended by some thirty or forty children ranging in age from six to sixteen. Boys and girls were educated together, not (it goes without saying) because of any belief in the desirability of coeducation, but because it was cheaper that way. Education consisted mainly of learning how to write Chinese characters. The children sat at little desks for hours at a time writing the same character over and over on a large sheet of paper until it and they were black with ink. Education was practical: pupils began by learning to write the characters used in local place names, gradually progressing to names of more distant spots, and then to common surnames. In this way they at least learned to address a parcel correctly, a matter of importance to a shopkeeper. Pupils who were able to continue their education beyond this stage were given instruction for two or three years in manuals of correct behavior which enjoined them to be dutiful to their parents and diligent in their work. The finishing touches of education for boys consisted of instruction in the Chinese classics, which they learned to pronounce aloud if not to understand. Girls were taught instead Japanese poetry and etiquette for young ladies. Such instruction, together with the use of the abacus, made up the bulk of the education offered to children of the merchant class. Children of the upper classes were given a more solid foundation in the literary and martial virtues, and children of the farmers remained illiterate.

Not all instruction came from the schools. The theater, for example, became in the seventeenth century another important factor in education. The merchants learned at the puppet theater or the Kabuki much about Japanese history—in somewhat distorted terms, it is true—and grew accustomed to the familiar tags of Chinese and Japanese poetry. Some plays also embodied religious teachings, and characters frequently mouthed speeches derived from the Confucian classics. The growth of a popular theater was followed by that of popular fiction, and a variety of novels, both frivolous and moralistic, began to beguile and sometimes to instruct a wider circle of readers than literature had ever reached before.

Vocational education was based chiefly on a system of apprenticeship. Society was divided into four classes—the samurai, the merchants, the artisans and the farmers—and apprenticeship differed according to the class. The samurai boy was trained in the use of weapons and hardened to physical endurance by his tutors. The boy of the merchant class (particularly a younger son), on the other hand, was likely to be sent as a boy of ten as a *detchi* (apprentice) to some other merchant's shop. When his parents bound him as an apprentice they had to guarantee that the boy would obey his new master with absolute devotion, and the boy was made aware of this responsibility. In return he was to be taught a trade, though the process was a long and indirect one. His first jobs as a *detchi* were often to help in the kitchen or merely to keep the ashtrays emptied, but gradually he came to be trusted enough for minor errands. The lowliness of his status is perhaps best indicated by the fact that until he was

106   Children learning Nō plays in Kanazawa declaim fifteenth-century poetry and move about in the grave, ceremonial manner prescribed in this ancient art.

107   Pretending it is night in a forest, these kindergarten children cover their eyes, and one little girl "sleeps" among the trees.

108   (Over) Brushwriting is an important part of the education of these children in a mountain village school, though the fountain pen is now more commonly used.

109   (Over) On the first school day of the new year, children are especially careful, believing that if they write well then they will write well the rest of the year.

110   (Over) Girls generally take care of their little sisters, even carrying them to school.

106   HIROSHI HAMAYA

107   KEN HEYMAN: RAPHO GUILLUMETTE

109

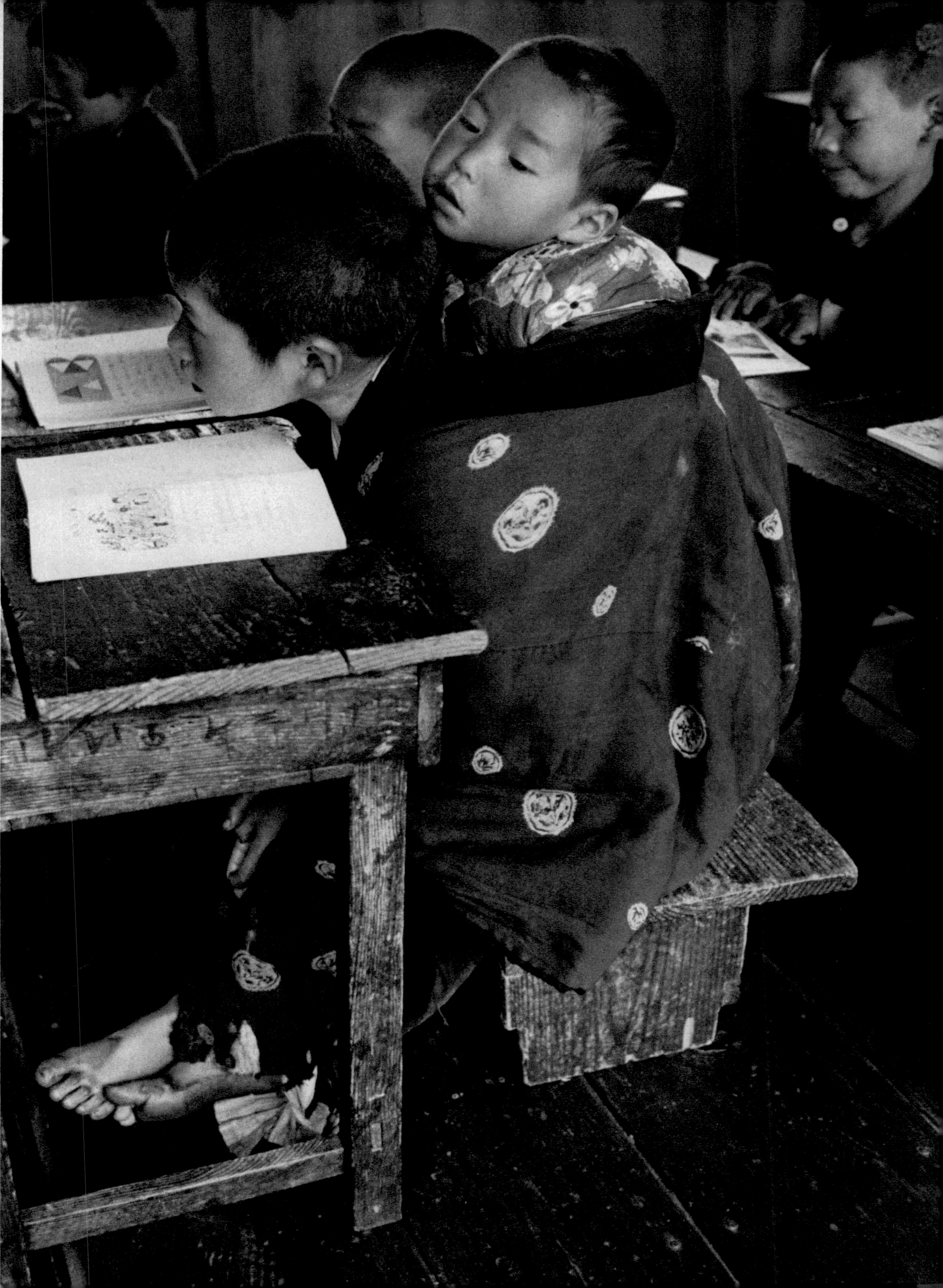

Tadahiko Hayashi: Chuokoron-sha

111

SHIGEICHI NAGANO: CHUOKORON-SHA

112

fifteen or so he was never called by name, but only "boy," "child," or the equivalent of "hey you!"

At fifteen, however, his promotion was signalized by his being given a kind of official nickname, and he was allowed for the first time to help with accounts and other business. This does not mean that he enjoyed much greater freedom: he was forbidden to smoke or drink, and every article of his clothing was prescribed to the last detail. Even his leisure time was strictly supervised by senior clerks who made sure that he spent his evening practicing his penmanship or the abacus. An especially promising *detchi* was rewarded by rapid advancement or preferred treatment, but for most young lads the life of a *detchi* was hard indeed. At nineteen or later—sometimes as late as forty—the boy graduated from *detchi* to shop assistant, an event marked by a celebration and presents from the entire household. He was now permitted to wear a formal kimono, to smoke and to wear *geta,* and given a more dignified name. He worked in the shop, entertaining customers or making entries in the ledger, sometimes taking the place of the master in business matters. If he continued to please in this capacity, his master might one day authorize him to set up a shop of his own, using the crest of the "main house." Sometimes the master bestowed his daughter on the young man as a final reward. The cycle was completed when the erstwhile *detchi,* established in business for himself, made life as difficult for his own *detchi* as it had once been for him. It is small wonder that this system was formally abolished in 1894 as "slave education."

Although the *detchi* is no longer a mainstay of business organizations, the system still prevails in many crafts and arts. Where it has fallen into abeyance some people lament the fact, saying that it spells the death of tradition. The young man who decides, for example, that he would like to make *sushi*—a popular delicacy of rice balls topped with horse-radish and raw fish—must go through an apprenticeship almost as long as a *detchi*'s. They say it takes eight or ten years to learn to make *sushi* properly. What this means in fact is that a boy spends the first two or three years delivering orders, another couple of years cleaning the kitchen, and still further years at slicing fish. Only after this long "training" is he shown how to mould the rice in the proper way into *sushi*. Any person reasonably clever with his hands can learn the art in a couple of months, yet because of the persistence of belief in the old educational system, the making of *sushi* is considered to be a difficult art which takes years to perfect.

Part of the slowness of the apprenticeship system may be laid to the jealousy shown by the established masters towards younger men, and part to their reluctance to admit that their art can quickly be acquired. Often an older man, far from helping promising newcomers, will subject them to severe physical punishments and place every possible stumbling-block in their path, ostensibly to test whether they really have an avocation for the art, but often to discourage

111 A modern high school classroom in Japan looks much like one in the West, though co-education at this level dates back only to the war

112 High school girls learn the tea ceremony, an accomplishment which every well-bred young lady is expected to master

them. A hierarchy among the disciples is common, and the master transmits the "secret traditions" of the art only to the chosen one. This close relationship between master and disciple seems to go back to the scholars of esoteric Buddhism. They insisted that (because only a very few people can understand the profound teachings of the Buddha) a master must be careful to transmit them only to the best qualified student. It may be imagined how desperately eager each disciple is to be accepted as the chosen one, if only because possession of the secret tradition enables him to become a full-fledged teacher himself. Every art has secrets that have never been committed to paper. When Japanese scholars in the eighteenth century first saw European scientific books, they were amazed especially to note that authors published all their findings, instead of jealously husbanding them within a school.

The prevalence of secret traditions brought about another feature of the old-style education: the many and distinct schools of every art. The first question one asks a friend today who is studying the Nô, for example, is the name of his school, and the same question might equally be asked of flower arrangement, painting, the tea ceremony, drum playing, cookery, archery, horseback riding or horoscope reading, and so on. Each school has its own traditions, traced back to a distant founder and believed to be the only true and unadulterated ones. Minute differences in procedure are clung to as the secret essence of the art, and before the student can obtain a licence from the head of his school, he must have learned each piece or arrangement exactly in the manner prescribed. Often, even after a student has faithfully attended a school for years, he will not be taught some of the secrets—how to twirl his brush slightly when making a certain stroke, or a feinting motion of his body which will confuse a fencing opponent. He will therefore spend years diligently imitating the style of his school unsuccessfully without knowing the little trick which would make things easy.

Survivals of the old style of education are surprisingly numerous and strong. Its failings are obvious. The painter's disciple who sweeps the floor for five years would learn more about painting if he had a brush instead of a broom in his hand. He would also progress more rapidly if all the secrets were taught him as a matter of course rather than as a special grace. Yet the musician who today proudly shows the scars in his scalp inflicted by a short-tempered master, and the actor who insists that no one born outside the profession can ever hope to learn it, also have a point. Only a person whose life is completely bound up with a traditional art can hope to learn it as a master should. The boy who grows up in a family of Nô actors hears rehearsals all day long even if he spends his time washing dishes in the kitchen, and he acquires an instinctive feeling for the right delivery of a line which cannot easily be taught. The apprentice who is so determined to become a puppet operator that he patiently endures the wounds and insults of his master, will develop greater perfection than another man to whom being a puppet operator is just another job. The old style of education was unenlightened, undemocratic and inefficient, but it produced masters whose likes will not be seen again.

THE PRE-WAR EDUCATION

Before the Meiji Restoration of 1868 there were no public schools and almost no modern education. The *terakoya* and the various schools for the samurai children offered training only in the classics, and though the pioneers of Western learning were beginning to agitate for an introduction of the new scientific knowledge, their influence was as yet minor. When the great political upheaval of the Restoration brought about the collapse of the feudal institutions and the abolition of the four classes of society, a new system of education became an immediate necessity.

Ambitious programs of education inspired by the examples of foreign countries were undertaken in the desire to make Japan equally strong and rich. In 1871 the Ministry of Education was established, and in the following year a school system was instituted along the lines of the French centrally controlled education. Plans called for the immediate erection of some 53,000 elementary schools, an enormous undertaking which could not be completely realized for many years. Even as late as 1902 only about half that number of schools had actually been built; nevertheless, both the effort and the results must be accounted prodigious. Not only did the new government face the problem of building schools and training teachers, but it had to determine a suitable content for education. Some experts favored a completely Western education which, they said, would permit Japanese children to catch up on the successes of modern civilization. Other people favored a compromise "combining the best of East and West." Among the common people, there were many opposed to the whole idea of compulsory education. Farmers often voiced the conviction that learning to use the abacus was quite enough schooling for their children, and saw no reason for teaching them difficult Chinese characters or Western mathematics. Resistance to the new education laws led in some cases to violence, and despite the efforts of the government to attract children to the new schools, attendance during the early days was less than thirty per cent. Even in the cities parents could often ill afford to allow their children to spend the whole day at school away from the shop, and withdrew them from the government schools entering them instead in easy-going *terakoya*. Official policy on education vacillated from liberal proposals conceived under American influence to Confucian injunctions on the importance of loyalty and filial piety as the cornerstones of education. In 1886 a school law was issued, which was modeled on German examples and highly nationalistic in flavor;

this was to become the basis for future Japanese education. The celebrated decree on education issued by the Emperor Meiji in 1890 emphasized the importance of Japanese traditions. It was to be repeated by millions of Japanese students for generations, despite the eagerness with which they were in fact turning to Western learning.

Some of the ambitious plans laid during the early Meiji Period required many years to fulfill, but compulsory education for all children became a reality, and in the space of a few years Japanese were trying to digest centuries of Western learning. The instructions issued to students in Toyama Prefecture in 1874 indicate the tenor of the new education. "The reason why the Western countries are all strong and prosperous is that their people are well-educated. The men of the West are neither gods nor Buddhas; their education is what has enabled them to invent the useful devices which have made their countries prosper. Unless we all take the greatest care, not only will we be laughed at by the foreigners, but we may well be made their servants."

The Japanese—whether out of fear of mocking foreigners or a more straight-forward desire to acquire useful knowledge—advanced with rapid strides. Before long they could boast not only the highest standard of literacy in all of Asia, but one comparable to that of European countries. The increase of literacy meant in turn a steadily growing audience for newspapers, magazines and books. Just as the statesmen of the early Meiji Period had planned, the Japanese commoners shook off the ignorance and illiteracy which had been their lot from time immemorial, and were enabled to help build the new Japan.

The educational system which eventually developed provided for elementary schools which were compulsory, followed by middle schools attended by many children in the cities and some in the country, and by high schools and universities intended for gifted students only. At the summit of the whole system stood the imperially established universities, particularly those in Tokyo and Kyoto, and these were the goals of every ambitious young man. Success in the government service—still, in the Confucian tradition, the most admired career—was dependent on a young man's graduation from one of the imperial universities, which therefore tended to produce highly-trained functionaries. More liberal traditions were represented by Waseda and Keiô, two private universities in Tokyo, which contributed greatly to both cultural and commercial development in Meiji Japan.

In order to gain admittance to any of the major universities a student had to have risen by regular stages from the best elementary school to the best middle school and the best high school in his part of the country. The relative standing of different schools was clearly known, and students diligently prepared to pass the entrance examinations in order to maintain their chances of advancement. Even six-year-olds took examinations for nursery school, and success in them was considered important, because it augured well for the

113 *Japanese medical science, among the most advanced in the world, is taught by up-to-date methods, including closed-circuit television*

114 *University students are often poor, and usually their lodgings are barely large enough for bedding and books. But almost any sacrifice is thought worthwhile for a university education*

113   JAPANESE CONSULATE GENERAL, NEW YORK

114

WERNER BISCHOF: MAGNUM

115

child's future. The boy who followed the orthodox path, eventually graduating from the First Middle School, the First High School and the Law Department of Tokyo University, could confidently expect a successful career. Unfortunately, however, the product of this system was often no more than a man with a talent for passing examinations based on factual knowledge. No imaginative understanding or ability to make practical judgments was expected. There are numerous stories of young men who memorized whole English dictionaries (eating each page after memorizing it so that the vocabulary would enter the blood) or who knew textbooks backwards.

115 *University students, a politically active group, gather in front of the Minami Theater in Kyoto to distribute leaflets.*

Although the object of the imperial universities was to produce useful, obedient public servants, it recognized the necessity of some break in the rigid discipline. This occurred in the high schools, a period when youths were expected to let their hair grow long and their fingernails get dirty and to wear ostentatiously ragged clothes. The First High School in Tokyo was especially noted for its Bohemianism. There was even a word, "dormitory rain," coined to describe the students urinating from their windows onto the street below. These students knew that this was the one period of freedom that the society was likely to allow them between childhood and old age. An educational system which fostered either complete conformity or complete eccentricity, and failed to encourage independent thought, must be held at least partly responsible for the ignominious acquiescence of its graduates to the militarists during the many cabinet crises of the 1930's. The typical graduate of the system was a man well equipped to carry out somebody else's orders.

The pre-war educational system was in a sense completely democratic. The examinations were open to all and admission was entirely on the basis of performance. No amount of influence could secure a student's admission to one of the imperial universities, and even the private universities maintained high standards. The total effect of the system tended however to be undemocratic, if only because it gave graduates of Tokyo University an absolute advantage for the rest of their careers over all other men. Of course, the fact that a young man was not a graduate of Tokyo University did not mean that he was doomed to perpetual failure, but he was always at a disadvantage. If he went into business, for example, he discovered that Tokyo graduates favored other Tokyo graduates in awarding contracts or in appointing new men to the company. The graduates of Tokyo University formed a powerful clique in the Diet and the bureaucracy.

Something of this feeling persists to this day. Most members of the post-war cabinets have been graduates of Tokyo University, as are about a quarter of the Diet members. In the academic world, the sense of superiority of Tokyo University men is so strong that they allow no graduates of other universities on their faculty. This helps to explain why students spend years cramming for the Tokyo University entrance examinations.

THE POST-WAR EDUCATION

The war had scarcely ended before Japanese educators, responding to the political changes, began to undertake educational reforms. Elementary school teachers, who a few months earlier had been preaching the necessity of absolute obedience to the Emperor, suddenly were singing the praises of democracy, to the bewilderment and sometimes the anger of the students. The Occupation authorities were soon ordering major changes in education, many of them actually those which Japanese teachers had long hoped for themselves. For example, compulsory education was extended to include middle school, for a total of nine years, and admission to high school no longer depended on examinations. This meant that instead of training pupils through most of their school careers to pass examinations, teachers could concentrate on giving them a good education. Only the entrance examinations of the leading universities were left as a grim reminder of the system which had prevailed, and an attempt was made to mitigate the disappointment of students who failed by establishing many more governmental and prefectural universities.

In order to break down the old notions of a "best" elementary school and so on, it was made obligatory for pupils to attend the school in their own district. As far as the instruction itself, the nationalistic emphasis was eliminated and the writing of the Japanese language—long the bugbear of the curriculum—much simplified. In place of the centrally organized, monolithic educational system which had insisted that every seventh-grade pupil in Japan at a given moment be reading the same page of the same textbook, regional and local educators were empowered to compile texts best suited to the needs of their students. Friendlier, less authoritarian relations between teachers and students were encouraged. The teachers, with the blessings of the Occupation authorities, formed unions intended to improve their material conditions. School boards similar to those in America were created. In other words, many features of American education were introduced in Japan in the belief that they would make the Japanese more democratic and independent.

Some American-inspired reforms, however, did not suit Japan, and others, the work of Americans whose experience was confined to small communities at home, could not be applied successfully to millions of Japanese teachers and students. The first flaring of anti-American sentiment after the war came in connection with the stubborn (but eventually unsuccessful) attempts of one American expert on education to force a revision of Japanese university charters. On the whole, however, the post-war changes in Japanese education were for the best. They succeeded only partly in their aims, but even this was admirable, especially in view of the reaction which later set in.

It did not take long for conservative Japanese opinion to begin nibbling at the structure of the new education. Traditional ideas of hierarchy made the

American insistence on the equality of high schools, for example, most uncongenial, and parents were soon trying to think of ways of circumventing the school district law so that they could enter their children in the "best" high school, the one from which admission to Tokyo University was most likely. Families moved in order to be in the right district, or a child was given in adoption to a relative who lived there. No sacrifice was considered excessive in order to place the child firmly within the new hierarchy. Gradually too an emphasis on examinations began to creep back into the teaching, and with it a proportional decrease of extracurricular activity, creative work, and sleep. Conservative educators began also to protest against the fact that Japanese history and geography were being neglected—that a Japanese child was more likely to know about Abraham Lincoln than about one of the great warriors of the Japanese past.

One by one the American-instituted reforms were brought under attack, often (ironically enough) by persons most friendly to America. On the other hand the most outspoken advocates of the American-style education included bitterly anti-American leftists. The government accused the teacher's union of being Communist-dominated, and the charge was not without foundation. On one occasion, for example, defiant teachers had run up a red flag over a school building. It became increasingly difficult to distinguish between teachers who were genuinely trying to instill democratic principles in their pupils by teaching them to question authority, rather than submit as in the past with blind adherence, and those who used the classroom as a platform for their anti-governmental sentiments. Liberal education was threatened from both the right and left: in some schools the principals reinstalled the Emperor's photograph and morning worship of it, while in others the students were encouraged to write essays denouncing American imperialism. Japanese educators began to talk of a "sandwich" in which the generation educated in the decade of liberalism was pressed by generations educated according to authoritarian principles.

The new education has many detractors, but even the most conservative parents must admit that their children are better informed than they were in many respects. The student of today, it is true, no longer memorizes dictionaries, but more often than before he learns to speak a foreign language. He may not lard his compositions with difficult Chinese allusions, but he organizes them better and can document them. He may be ignorant of the achievements of Japanese heroes, but he has learned to see Japanese history as a part of world history instead of as an unique entity. Most important of all, he has learned to respect a variety of opinions on any subject, an attitude which is anathema to any totalitarian system, but which once possessed is not easily abandoned.

Chapter IX

THE WORLD OF PLEASURE

THE VISITOR to Japan may easily form the impression that the Japanese are inordinately fond of amusements. Block after block paralleling the Ginza, in Tokyo, is occupied by bars, nightclubs and pinball-machine establishments, and many other areas of the city are given over to the world of pleasure. The facilities range from squalid little bars crowded to capacity by a bare half-dozen customers (and a like number of raucous-voiced hostesses) to the elegant spaciousness of the large geisha houses. Furtive-looking men loiter in the streets, eager to escort tourists to forbidden entertainments, and all-night cafés cater to couples who wish to sit for long hours in the dark. In the countryside, of course, the amusements are healthier if less varied, but in many of the small cities one can find dim replicas of Tokyo night life. Kyoto, a city with few industries, depends for its prosperity largely on the money spent by out-of-towners on pleasures too dear for the thrifty natives—a dinner costing an average man's monthly wages or a party at a famous "teahouse" running to hundreds of dollars.

Almost every kind of entertainment known in the West can also be found in Japan. The most characteristically Japanese (though too expensive to be enjoyed by any but the very rich) is that of the geishas. These ladies, indeed, are so famous in the West that a picture of one is almost as much a symbol of Japan as Mount Fuji, though not one much relished by the Japanese themselves. However familiar the geisha has become through stories and photographs, most Westerners nevertheless have no idea what is in store for them when they are invited to a geisha party. Most—whatever they expect— are disappointed. A visit to one of the famous houses is a memorable experience, but its pleasures are not those commonly conjured up by the word geisha. For one thing,

116 *Every January 17th at the Bonden Festival in Akita, young men boisterously carry decorated poles through the snow. The belief is that the gods use them to get from heaven to earth*

117 *(Over) Before a sumô bout, the Japanese style of wrestling, the wrestler "salutes" with his leg. At the right, looking on gravely, is the referee*

118 *(Over) A geisha carries a fan with the picture of a favorite sumô wrestler*

119 *(Over) The elaborate belt and loincloth indicates the rank of champion*

117   SHELDON A. BRODY

118   HORACE BRISTOL

119   WERNER BISCHOF: MAGNUM

120   HIROSHI HAMAYA

121   DENNIS STOCK: MAGNUM

a man is not at liberty to visit a geisha house whenever the mood for feminine companionship seizes him. An introduction is necessary, and thus the very fact of being present in a leading establishment makes the occasion a social one—a matter of greater importance to Japanese men than to foreigners. The geisha house itself is hardly more than a beautiful building. No geishas regularly live there; food is not prepared; and customers do not spend the night. The host who wishes to entertain there indicates the number of geishas and *maiko* (girls who have yet to become full-fledged geishas) whom he wishes to engage. The fees for geishas vary according to their popularity, but all are high, and a party attended by four or five geishas ranks as a major extravagance. Most geisha parties are far too expensive for an ordinary individual, and must therefore be ticked off to "company expenses."

The newspapers have raised a considerable fuss over revelations that some of the leading politicians of recent years have attended parties at which a dozen or more geishas waited on the guests, but the entertainment at a geisha house tends to be rather sedate. A dance or two performed by a *maiko* to the accompaniment of a samisen and a singer is followed by the dances of the older geishas. The foreigner who imagines that a geisha's dance is particularly seductive will be disappointed. The *maiko* dances with a certain coquetry as she mimes the suitable actions for the four seasons of Kyoto, or whatever the subject of her dance may be, but she is amply clothed in many-layered kimonos, and her face is set throughout in a conventionalized simper. The dances of the geishas themselves—especially in Kyoto—are severe and almost masculine, for they are derived from the Nô plays. The best dancers are women in their forties who are by no means remarkable beauties; some geishas continue to perform until their sixties, and one went on till she was 101.

Before and after the dances the *maiko* and geishas surround the guest, urging saké on him and daintily accepting drinks from his cup. They sit very close to the guest, often pressing their knee against his side. They may from time to time strike him playfully on the wrist, but physical contact usually does not go much beyond this point. The conversation (depending on the guest) may be perfectly decorous or border on the obscene. Geishas are traditionally supposed to be fine conversationalists, though few today live up to the tradition. One may indeed get the impression that the guest bears the responsibility for entertaining the geisha. Business matters are sometimes discussed at geisha parties—their justification in terms of office expenses is that they help to put prospective clients in a favorable mood—but aimless banter is the order of the evening.

The word *geisha* literally means "artist," and girls who aspire to this profession must undergo a lengthy training in singing, dancing and samisen-playing. They are expected also to divert guests with their wit and by little tricks with a fan or saké cups. The modern geisha may boast a smattering of English for the entertainment of foreign visitors, and an acquaintance with

120–121 *Immense crowds gather to watch the regular* sumô *matches in Tokyo. The ring is under a roof resembling that of a Shinto shrine, and the spectators sit on matting spread out in little boxes.*

political and literary gossip for Japanese dignitaries. Geishas, in the cities at least, are usually the daughters of other geishas, and grow up in a quarter where the sound of the samisen is never out of hearing. Formerly a girl became a *maiko* when she was eleven or twelve, but the new school laws now make it impossible for her to take up the profession until she is about fifteen. Connoisseurs complain that the young geisha today lacks the charms which a longer apprenticeship used to give her.

A *maiko* is nonetheless a lovely sight as she trips down the street, her elaborate coiffure tinkling with silver pins and flowers, her face and neck painted white, her body swathed in a brilliantly colored kimono tied with a brocaded hanging sash, her feet encased in delicately rounded *geta*. In the room where she dances she is like an animated, exquisite toy, hardly given to speech and seldom displaying any interest beyond keeping her guests' cups filled. Souvenirs of Kyoto are usually decorated with pictures of *maiko* standing on bridges or under wisteria boughs, and they are the idols of the countless thousands of schoolgirls in middy blouses who visit Kyoto on school outings.

Such recognition of their profession must be pleasing to the *maiko,* but with the increase in the possibilities for beautiful girls to make a career in the movies, as models or as receptionists, many daughters of geishas are turning from their mothers' profession. A *maiko* normally becomes a geisha at about the age of eighteen, though some choose to leave the profession altogether and a few become prostitutes.

The difference between a geisha and a prostitute—always a matter of lively interest to foreigners—has not always been clear even to Japanese. The first geishas (in the eighteenth century) were dancers—either women or men— and were called in to entertain at parties which might also be graced by prostitutes. This original distinction between geisha and prostitute tended to become blurred in later years, but in 1872 the government enacted laws designed to make sure that only genuine "artists" were permitted to appear in geisha houses. The position of the geishas was again debated after the war. The military authorities had made the geishas "comforters" for their officers, and many advocates of progress therefore favored total abolition of the institution. Instead, the geishas were authorized to perform again as dancers and singers, and today the women at the recognized geisha establishments in the cities are definitely artists; some, indeed, are too old to be anything else.

The geisha, however, almost invariably has a patron, a man to whom she is supposed to be faithful. She may bestow her favors on other men occasionally, particularly if they are rich enough and very determined, but there is an immense difference between such a woman and a prostitute obliged to accept any man who pays. One reason why many geishas yield to rich men is that they are usually in debt. Their work obliges them to buy many extremely costly clothes, and other extravagances are expected of them. The terms of

122 *The Japanese play baseball with skill, fanatical enthusiasm, and, like these shipyard workers, even during lunch hour.*

123 *Many big companies have baseball teams. Here a cheer leader whips up enthusiasm for the Columbia Record team.*

122

Werner Bischof: Magnum

123

Dennis Stock: Magnum

124

125

MARC RIBOUD: MAGNUM

MARC RIBOUD: MAGNUM

126

HIROSHI HAMAYA

their contracts with the geisha houses range from a nominal connection to almost complete subservience, but few geishas escape heavy debts. A patron is necessary also to help the geisha eventually to open a "teahouse" or restaurant of her own. Geishas sometimes marry their patrons and lead matronly lives ever after, but something of their old profession often clings to them as a memento of former days. The closest parallel to the geisha in the West is, perhaps, the stage actress.

The celebrated red-light districts were closed by law in 1958 throughout Japan, largely as the result of pressure from women's groups. In recent years these sections (especially those rebuilt after the war) had become ugly and sordid, in no way suggesting their role in the past, when they served as a center of Japanese city life and culture.

One can still get a glimpse of a more glamorous past by visiting one of the former brothels, the Sumiya in Kyoto, a magnificent building over three hundred years old, decorated with superb woodwork in each room and paintings by distinguished former customers. Only gentlemen were privileged to visit the Sumiya; sword marks on the wooden pillars tell where samurai once quarrelled, and the proprietor nostalgically relates how formerly even great actors were refused admission because they were not of gentle birth.

Today the last few of the great courtesans (*tayu*) still perform their traditional presentation ceremony in the Sumiya for the benefit of tourists. At night, in a large room lit only by candles, the tourists of today, like the samurai of bygone years, sit at low tables while a woman attendant takes her place and kneels by a door at the opposite end of the room. Suddenly the black rectangle of the door is filled with the glints of the gold thread of a kimono, and the flashes of silver ornaments in a woman's hair, caught in the flickering candlelight. The attendant calls out the courtesan's name in high-pitched, weird-sounding syllables, and with a rustle of silks she moves into the room. Silently she performs the ritual gestures of her ceremony with the symbolic saké cup, then she slowly crosses the room, hardly more than an apparition, to bow before the guests. Viewed from closer up she is little less ghostly: her face and hands are covered with thick white paint; her massive coiffure is burdened with heavy ornaments; and as she sits her robes spread out around her like a pavilion.

In former days the *tayu* stood at the top of an elaborate hierarchy of prostitutes, and she was considered a great lady, to be approached with awe by most commoners. Much of the literature of the seventeenth and eighteenth centuries is concerned with love affairs between young men and prostitutes, unhappy romances destined to end in double suicides. The Confucian code which governed society insisted that wives be obedient, docile and silent—all good things in a woman, but not very exciting. Men were therefore apt to seek more amusing companionship with prostitutes, and their relations were condoned providing that they did not interfere with the man's family duties.

124-125 *The beaches are popular with young people who favor the Western fashion, and old ladies who stick to traditional ways.*

126 *At a hot spring in a northern rural area, farmers and their wives bathe together. As the result of Western influence, mixed bathing has become much less common than a century ago when it startled Commodore Perry and his men.*

In recent years, fewer and fewer houses attempted to keep up the old traditions of elegance. Rows of brothels, blocks long, were a feature of Japanese cities, and the cries of the women standing in the doorways, luring in the customers, were part of the night music. European writers often praised the Japanese attitude towards prostitution, contrasting it with more hypocritical attitudes found elsewhere, and noting how the prostitute kept her fiancé's picture in her cubicle (a sign that she was not lost to society), or how straightforwardly sexual desires were gratified. Thinly-disguised subterfuges for brothels are today much in evidence: "hotels" which advertise rooms by the hour; "restaurants" with back rooms into which customers frequently disappear; "bars" where hostesses go far beyond the call of friendliness.

Despite the persistence of Confucian morality, the Japanese tend to be permissive in sexual matters, as many foreign visitors are quick to discover. Few moral restrictions are imposed on what gets into print. The railway newsstands, for example, offer impressive displays of erotic magazines, and even novels by major authors written for a general Japanese public may include passages which could not be printed in an English translation. Some years ago, it is true, a trial over the publication of an unexpurgated Japanese translation of *Lady Chatterley's Lover* resulted in a fine for the translator, but this was most unusual. Undisputedly pornographic works are sold everywhere. The important place held in Japanese culture by erotic works of literature and art is a testimony to the long-standing partiality for this type of amusement. A similarly indulgent attitude towards sex is found in the bars, which offer not only liquor but the company of numerous young women, whose accustomed place is more frequently next to the customer than behind the bar. The pleasure of such company is so widely recognized as a male privilege that some Tokyo unions have recently demanded as "fringe benefits" an allowance to permit regular visits to these establishments!

Coffee shops are also extremely popular, particularly with the younger set. Some feature recordings of classical music, played either by request or carefully determined by the owner. For the price of a cup of coffee a student may sit through a cycle of Bruckner symphonies or a Shostakovitch festival. The waitresses at such coffee shops, however, are studiously indifferent to their customers, as if to establish the difference between themselves and bar girls.

Other entertainments popular with all classes of Japanese include dramatic presentations and sports. The serious varieties of theatricals will be discussed in the chapter devoted to the creative arts, but some others are of questionable artistic merit. The strip-tease shows, so popular since the end of the war, and the many kinds of burlesque and vaudeville acts regularly fill large theaters in the cities at a time when the traditional dramatic arts have fared poorly, inspiring numerous cynical remarks on the tastes of the post-war Japanese.

Some spectacles, like the fireworks on the river in Tokyo, have a long tradition behind them; others, like baseball, are quickly building a new orthodoxy. The standings of the different baseball clubs and the batting averages of the players are virtually required knowledge of every businessman, and people who show up late for appointments are easily forgiven if their tardiness has been occasioned by a baseball game. Not only are the professional teams followed with the keenest interest, but even the annual high school champion-ships attract immense crowds and the results are displayed as prominently as World Series scores in the United States. The results of college baseball games make the headlines. The rivalry between Waseda and Keiô Universities is so celebrated that a special noun, *Sokeisen,* designates baseball games played bet-ween the two schools. Most large companies have baseball teams, some ranking as "major leaguers," and the president of a firm may appear in his office with a bandaged arm, the result of an overenthusiastic slide.

The Japanese fondness for baseball has been explained on the basis of its suitability to the Japanese physique: it requires neither great height nor brawn, and gives play to native swiftness and dexterity. Paradoxically enough, however, the traditional Japanese wrestling called *sumô* is also considered to be peculiarly well suited to the Japanese physique, though it places a great pre-mium on height and brawn. *Sumô* is a very ancient sport, traditionally dating back 1500 years or more. Even if we do not accept this figure as literally true, its long popularity is unquestioned. *Sumô* was frequently performed in the presence of the emperor and, despite various ups and downs in the course of the centuries, maintained its place as the Japanese sport par excellence.

Its darkest moments came after the Meiji Restoration, when as part of the general campaign against nakedness—humiliating in the eyes of foreigners—*sumô* was entirely banned. The *sumô* wrestlers are not actually naked—they wear an elaborate loincloth—but the authorities of the time were so fearful that foreigners might think the Japanese savages that they lumped *sumô* together with snake-charming as undesirable entertainments. One writer of 1876 put it, "*Sumô* is the kind of sport indulged in by barbarous, uncivilized peoples, not by cultured nations. It is obvious that a country which is progressing towards civilization and enlightenment will prize knowledge and virtue, and despise the display of physical force." Not long afterwards, however, *sumô* was again permitted, partly at least because of the exploits of former *sumô* wrestlers in behalf of the Imperial cause during the rebellion of 1877.

Ever since that time *sumô* has maintained its popularity, despite increasing competition from baseball, "pro wrestling," swimming and other foreign sports. Small boys in the street imitate the forty-eight classical attacking moves of *sumô,* and teams compete at high schools and universities. *Sumô* is neverthe-less primarily a spectator sport, unlike *judo,* Japanese fencing (*kendo*) or even baseball. Enormous crowds gather to witness the ceremonial fifteen-day tournaments in Tokyo and Osaka, and many millions more follow the bouts by radio and television or through the newspapers; the popularity of *sumô* today is, in fact, largely a product of the mass media.

Sumô matches begin early in the morning and continue until evening, but only during the last few hours do wrestlers from "within the curtain"—the seeded athletes—appear. The audience consequently tends to arrive late. It is predominantly male, but includes wives and daughters of *sumô* fans and geishas. Seats are in little boxes where one squats Japanese style, first removing one's shoes. Tickets are generally bought through teahouses which supply refreshments and cushions. People of all classes of society and ages mingle.

A *sumô* match still preserves something of its ritual character. The huge wrestlers (some weigh close to 300 pounds), girded in elaborate belts and with their long hair tied in topknots, perform stylized prayers and limbering-up movements. They scatter salt, purifying the ring, then approach each other tentatively several times as if to begin the bout. Each time, however, they are waved back by the referee, a bearded man in pastel robes and court hat, looking rather like a Shinto priest, who waves a curious square fan to give commands. Finally the wrestling begins, two immense, powerful men pushing and lunging. The object is to force one's opponent either to step out of the ring or else to touch the ground with some other part of his body than the soles of his feet. A bout seldom takes more than a couple of minutes.

The standings of the wrestlers depend on their performances in the tournaments. A man with a perfect, or nearly perfect, record may shoot up from the ranks of "within the curtain" wrestlers to one of the three graded titles at the top, and eventually he may become a *yokozuna,* and wear the horizontal rope-skirt of the grand champion. Once a man reaches this eminence he is no longer subject to the vicissitudes of other wrestlers, but reigns at the top until his retirement. Wrestlers often start studios (*heya*) of their own for training younger men. *Sumô* wrestlers are for the most part sturdy country youths who cheerfully lead lives of an almost dedicated simplicity. Not surprisingly, in view of its long history, the organization of *sumô* today retains many feudal elements.

It is rather strange, on the other hand, that *sumô* for all its traditional qualities should owe so much of its present popularity to modern media, which otherwise favor quiz programs and popular songs as elsewhere in the world. However, two other purely Japanese entertainments, *rakugo* and *naniwabushi,* have become radio and television favorites despite their antiquated flavor. *Rakugo* is a kind of storytelling, usually delivered by a man who sits in formal Japanese clothes in the middle of the stage. The language is old-fashioned, and the anecdotes themselves may date back hundreds of years. Perhaps the most famous *rakugo* is that of the man afraid of *manju,* a kind of cake. A certain man is badgered by his friends into telling them what he most fears, and finally confesses that he dreads nothing so much as a *manju.* The friends, delighted to have elicited this secret, place a small *manju* by his pillow to frighten him when

127 *Fishing is popular with tired businessmen, who flee the overcrowded cities for crystal-clear rivers in the mountains.*

128 *(Over) At the annual festival at Saidaiji Temple in Okayama, a sacred stick is thrown among thousands of naked men, who struggle furiously for it, believing it will bring prosperity*

129   SHELDON A. BRODY

130

SHELDON A. BRODY

he awakens, but when the man opens his eyes he at once eats the *manju* with great gusto. He then says, "A good cup of tea is what I'm most afraid of now." This story is said to be ultimately of Chinese origin, but many *rakugo* deal specifically with the life of the old Edo (Tokyo), and have in fact been a way in which newcomers to the city have learned something of its traditions. *Rakugo* is performed in small theaters in Tokyo today, but thanks to the radio, has become familiar throughout the country.

Naniwabushi is considered to be an Osaka art. It is a long recitation performed to a somewhat musical accompaniment of a samisen, and delivered in a strained, tortured voice. The subject matter is usually the prowess of gallant commoners during the Tokugawa Period. Ever since the end of the nineteenth century these ballads have held an immense appeal for the lower classes, and even today are their favorite kind of radio program. Most of the stories are gloomy and rather Buddhist in tone, not very promising qualities for mass entertainment, one might suppose. However, most Japanese, for all their love of amusement, seem to be happier with a good cry than a good laugh. Intellectuals, on the other hand, admire *rakugo* and despise the *naniwabushi*. As early as 1908 one critic wrote, "The popularity of *naniwabushi* is itself a proof that the Japanese have no musical culture." Certainly the samisen accompaniment is hardly more than trimming, and the sound of the reciter's voice, a distillation of everything which Western listeners find most trying in oriental music, is distressing even to educated Japanese. For the mass of the Japanese, however, *naniwabushi* recitations, evoking nostalgic memories of their country's past, are more likely to arouse heartfelt tears than the most accomplished tragedy in a modern idiom.

Some of the famous *naniwabushi* are about chivalrous gamblers, a profession with a long history in Japan. In the ancient records gambling is mentioned as the diversion (if not profession) of all classes. Dice games have maintained their popularity since those times, and card games, introduced to Japan in the seventeenth century by the Dutch (the Japanese word *karuta* is derived from the Dutch *kaart*) exist in many varieties. Eighteenth-century prints show not only courtesans and rakes but nuns, priests and grave Confucian scholars busily gambling at cards. While gambling is by no means a mania in Japan, games of chance have been popular even in conservative homes ever since the Meiji Restoration. Some require a knowledge of a collection of poetry, others are very refined indeed, like the betting on song-thrushes said to have been popular in Kyoto. In the latter game, a dwarf plum tree in blossom is placed in the middle of a large room, and at a signal the owners of the song-thrushes release the birds from their cages. The owner of the first bird to alight on the flowering tree wins the bet. An account from about 1900 tells of less aesthetic gambling games—of Tokyo housewives paying their shop clerks to join in card parties, or of farmers' wives obliged to spend days in their neighbor's fields working

129 *One of the pleasures of a Japanese festival is getting a little tipsy. A gentleman, in formal Japanese attire and derby, has lost his* geta *(wooden clog).*

130 *The ancient and complicated game of Go is a favorite with both young and old.*

off gambling debts. Some games were imported from China: *chiha* swept the country in the 1890's, and mahjong since the war has tempted many white-collar workers and other people of modest means to spend their nights at a gaming table. Horse-racing and bicycle-racing furnish many Japanese with the excuse to make bets, and there are also cock fights, dog fights, bull fights and miscellaneous other animal combats. Of course the vast majority of those who place bets are not professional gamblers likely to be celebrated in future *naniwabushi*. Some of the latter are still to be seen, often distinguishable by the tattooing which seems to be a mark of the profession.

Games of skill are also popular diversions, particularly with older people. *Go* (a complicated game in which one attempts to surround the pieces of one's opponent) and *shôgi* (a game rather resembling chess) both boast an elaborate hierarchy of masters, and newspaper columns are devoted to them. Such games are favorite distractions for travelers, an important fact in a country where so many people are constantly traveling.

Trains and busses, though numerous, are always crowded, and the ownership of automobiles is no longer restricted to the upper classes. The school excursion, a traditional feature of Japanese education, is often the first taste of travel for Japanese children. Classes of mischievous boys and giggling girls are guided by their teachers to Kyoto or Tokyo for three or four days. During the times of year popular with excursionists the streets of the famous cities are black with the uniforms of schoolchildren. Some pupils (and some adults on similar tours) record every word uttered by their guides in little notebooks, but the pleasure of travel has little to do with such gleanings. Travel means first of all to visit places designated as "famous places," and secondly to buy for people at home the souvenirs designated as "famous products."

The favorite destinations for many travelers are the hot springs with which Japan is amply favored. There are still hot springs in the mountains where ordinary folk go for the pleasure of bathing in the therapeutic waters with their friends, but any hot spring within striking distance of a large city has by now been exploited by clusters of elaborate hotels where the benefits of the waters are likely to be offset by the liquor and other diversions afforded. Men generally visit hot springs without their wives, and the tedium of long evening hours is dissipated for them by the local geishas, who are usually somewhat inferior to their city sisters in talent and morals.

Those who cannot afford to go to hot springs have at least the pleasure of the public bath. The Japanese are a cleanly people, and the main purpose of bathing is obviously to wash away the perspiration and dirt, but the bathhouse means more than washing. It is a center of communal activity where one can meet one's neighbor man-to-man with none of the artificial trappings of society. A book written about 1850 tells us, "It is in accordance with the natural principles of Heaven and Earth that all men—high and mighty or humble alike—

131 *A professional dancer poses for a familiar kind of picture.*

132 *(Over) The dances of geishas are very formal; the accompaniment is provided by the three-stringed samisen.*

133 *(Over) Guests leaving a tea-house put on their shoes while the geishas bow thanks.*

134 *(Over) This fashionable tea ceremony in Kanazawa preserves little of the austerity that tradition requires but is aesthetically quite pleasing.*

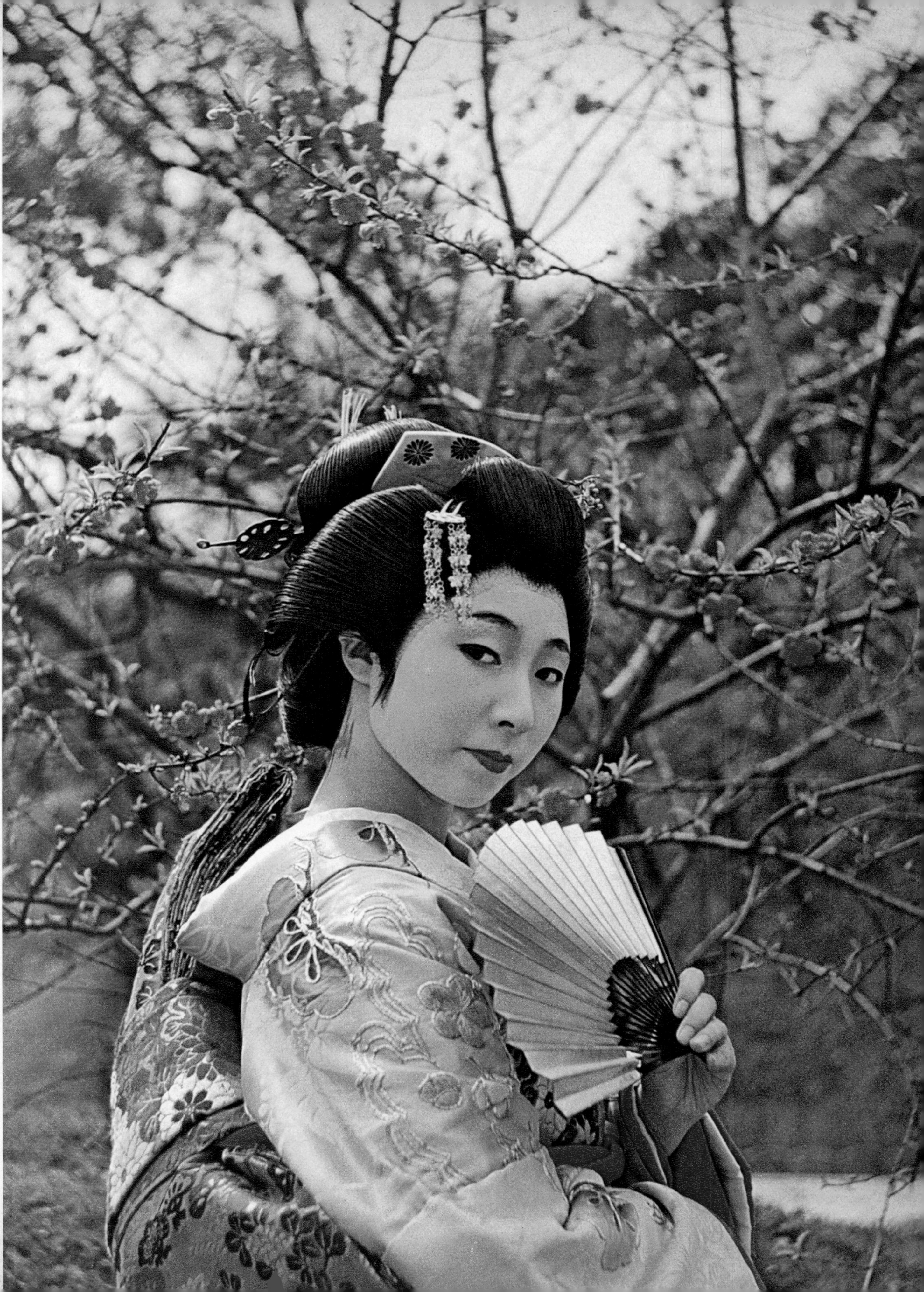

Eliot Elisofon

132   Dennis Stock: Magnum

133

134

135

136

must strip themselves naked when they take a bath. The samurai who wears two swords, the doctor with his silken robes, the lackey, the housewife, the priest, the spoiled child—all become as newborn babes and are freed of hatred and desire. When in the clear water, purifying themselves of the dust of desire and the sorrows of the world, how is one to tell which man is master and which servant, both being naked? An old man who hates the Buddha may unconsciously invoke his name as he steps into the boiling tub. The reckless cavalier, reduced to nakedness, learns the meaning of shame as he covers his privates. Even if a bucket of hot water is dumped over some bold warrior's head he must endure it patiently, for he is aware how crowded the place is, and he must stoop and apologize when he passes through the entrance. Does this not demonstrate the virtues of the bathhouse?"

135 *The strip-tease is seriously discussed by Japanese as a kind of modern art, and spectators assume a properly respectful air.*

Instances of the Japanese partiality for bathing may be found in the old literature, and travelers from abroad were invariably struck by the institution. A Korean envoy who visited Kyoto in 1430 was so impressed by Japanese bathhouses that on his return to his country he urged his government in vain to establish similar ones. The early Christian missionaries took a less favorable view of frequent baths, and restricted Japanese converts to one a week. The artist who accompanied Commodore Perry to Japan drew a sketch of mixed bathing in Shimoda which gained such notoriety that some editions of the account of Perry's expedition were suppressed in America. Today the little museum of sexual curiosa established in a Shimoda temple is enhanced by an enormously magnified reproduction of the forbidden illustration. Unsavory anecdotes about bath attendants, and what happens in ill-lighted bathhouses when there is mixed bathing, abound in Japanese literature, but the pleasures of the bathhouse are normally quite innocent.

136 *"Coffee, beer and girls" are offered at this bar, called the New Yorker. There are thousands like it in Tokyo.*

Most of the present amusements of the average Japanese—sporting contests, theatricals, storytellers, the bar, the bathhouse—have a long history. Photography is one of the few entirely new pleasures of modern life. Obviously the camera's popularity is not confined to Japan—the American with two cameras dangling around his middle is a common enough sight. But the Japanese have made the camera an almost indispensable feature of any event slightly removed from the commonplace; it is as if a meeting, a party or a visit has not really occurred until it has been photographed. Japan is a cameraman's paradise: there is hardly an event, however solemn, where amateur photographers are not free to fight their way to the front to snap a picture. *Maiko* may be hired to pose in front of temple gateways in their finery, and there are organized excursions with models.

Some diversions of the Japanese—fishing, mountain climbing, philately, dog raising and the like—differ little from their counterparts elsewhere; others belong to the world of the religious festivals; still others to the many manifestations of the creative life of Japan.

Chapter X

JAPAN THE CREATOR

THE HISTORIES of some countries might be written without giving more than a cursory glance at their artistic achievements; that of Japan, on the other hand, might more easily omit the names of emperors and descriptions of rebellions than neglect art, poetry and aesthetic life. It is true that the Japanese have a proverb, *hana yori dango*—meaning literally, "dumplings rather than flowers"—the outlook, one might think, of a people who knows the value of material things. Yet flowers are more characteristic of Japan than dumplings or, for that matter, than the stratagems of politics and finance.

The greatest work of Japanese literature, the eleventh-century *Tale of Genji,* gives an extensive portrait of court society with hardly a mention in thousands of pages of political events, let alone of anything so innocently materialistic as dumplings. The histories of old Japan are sprinkled with poetry and do not begrudge a chapter or two for an account of moon-viewing or a description of ancient gardens.

Life was certainly not a matter of flowers for the peasants, but, judging by the old folk songs, something of the aesthetic preoccupations of the aristocracy seems nevertheless to have been communicated even to them. Not only have most Japanese, regardless of class, welcomed the arts, but an ability to create works of art, or at least to perform them, has always been more or less assumed of every educated person. In the times of the *Tale of Genji* the ability to dash off a poem of one's own composition in an elegant hand was obligatory in a lover, and poetic talent was equally valuable as a means of gaining political advancement. Grizzled warriors were not embarrassed to perform the steps of a ceremonial dance or to play the flute. Even as late as the war of 1941–1945, many generals and admirals found the leisure to write verses about cherry blossoms and other time-honored themes.

137 *White Heron Castle in Himeji, completed in 1610, is the finest and best preserved in Japan. It has withstood the assaults both of soldiers and advocates of modernization.*

ELIOT ELISOFON

Japan Export Trade Promotion Agency

There has been no defection from this cult of beauty in the centuries since the *Tale of Genji,* despite the cruel disasters which mark Japanese history. At the end of the fifteenth century, for example, even while the city of Kyoto was being ravaged by civil warfare, a few miles away in his Silver Pavilion the shogun, Yoshimasa, was devoting most of the state revenues to aesthetic pleasures, including the tea ceremony and the new style of landscape painting.

Patronage of this kind was necessary in the development of some arts, but credit for their discovery often belonged with the common people. Again and again we find this sequence: a new kind of poetry or dramatic entertainment wins popularity among the common people; its aesthetic possibilities are recognized and eagerly exploited by professional poets and artists with court patronage; and it is then developed by them into an art which may eventually be shared by the entire nation. The *haiku,* today the most popular Japanese verse form, in the seventeenth century represented a revolt against the stereotypes of the older poetry; before long, however, professionals were refining the *haiku* and codifying its properties; today the daily newspapers feature *haiku* columns, dozens of monthly magazines are devoted exclusively to this poetry, and only a very dull Japanese is incapable of composing one.

Many traditional Japanese arts have shown an astonishing resistance to the movies, radio, television and other mass entertainments, though in some cases they have been preserved by only a handful of men. At New Year people still compose the classical *tanka* poetry in thirty-one syllables to a subject set by the Emperor; others learn the sing-song fashion of chanting Japanese renderings of ancient Chinese poetry; and little groups still write linked-verse, an art which most Japanese believe perished years ago. Not even the entertainments mentioned in the *Tale of Genji* have vanished: a few men in pastel robes and nodding gauzy hats still play Genji's style of football, the object of which is for all players to join in keeping the white deerskin ball in the air— a feature which makes the exponents of this game prefer it to competitive sports. Perfume-blending, another antique pastime, is today the avocation of elegant Tokyo matrons, while calligraphy continues to rank as a major art. The widespread use of the fountain-pen has made Japanese letters less of an aesthetic delight than in former days, but one may still be favored occasionally with a note brushed on sheets of paper of contrasting shades artfully pasted together to form a single long scroll, or on stationery embellished by delicately tinted flowers of the season. Even the young man who scorns the "feudal" culture of the past will feel rather ashamed not to be able to inscribe his name decently with a brush when he registers at the university or signs the guest book at the door of an art exhibition.

Opposition to the past is, however, extremely strong, particularly among the younger artists. The young potter may be compelled to produce conventional

197

bowls and cups in order to make a living, but he is likely to spend his spare time experimenting. He may choose to produce free-form pottery bristling with irregular knobs and bumps; and he will consider it a compliment to be told that his creation looks more like metal than pottery, for, he says, metal is more characteristic of our machine age. As far as he is concerned, the traditional forms were all perfected in the distant past and leave no room for improvements. To reproduce them, he says, is hardly better than hack work, and no more stimulating to his imagination than modern Western sculptors find the copying of Greek statues of Apollo or centaurs.

Almost all practitioners of the traditional arts desire either to liberate themselves from the past or at least to rediscover it in their own fashion. The painters of the so-called Japanese style use the customary pigments and paint on silver and gold paper, but their subjects, likely as not, are abstractions or Parisian scenes. Modern calligraphers deliberately distort the Chinese characters and choose for their texts translations of a stanza by Rainer Maria Rilke or the last words of Thomas Mann, instead of the traditional poetry or quotations from the sages. The directors of the puppet theater turn their backs on the immense repertory of rarely performed traditional works in order to stage *Hamlet* or *Madame Butterfly*—with disastrous results. The designer of kimono fabrics scornfully rejects the "Seven Grasses of Autumn" and other familiar motifs in favor of Egyptian frieze figures or geometrical patterns. The *haiku* poet in his revolt against conventional prosody may disregard altogether the length of his lines or even claim that a one-line statement is a *haiku*. Such a poet will probably treat with contempt anyone who adheres to the old rules, much in the way that a modern American poet will reject someone who follows the principles of nineteenth-century poetic diction. Even the man who insists that he does not deviate from the prescribed traditions, is probably unable to restrain himself from adding a few modern "improvements."

The foreigner may bewail such restlessness and wish that the Japanese would "stick to what they do best," but the reluctance of Japanese artists to allow themselves to be bound by tradition is itself the best sign of the vitality of the arts. A Japanese painter is perfectly well aware that if he draws pines and temples set in misty mountains he has an infinitely better chance of selling his work than if he does a large abstraction in angry colors. Nevertheless he feels that he must not betray his art by pandering to commercialism. In any case, as a serious artist he has no real choice: no matter how dextrous he may be, any work painted in a traditional vein is likely to be completely dead when it comes from the brush of a painter whose heart and mind are occupied by the terrifying realities of contemporary life. Fortunately the Japanese have not been paralyzed by the problem of reconciling tradition and change, and in painting, literature, the theater, and the other arts we find an intensity of activity which might well be the envy of many countries.

139 *The ferocious guardian at the gate of Todaiji Temple in Nara are benevolent; they were made to seem ugly to scare away evil spirits. Standing twenty-eight feet high, this 750-year-old figure is the largest wooden statue in the world*

WERNER BISCHOF: MAGNUM

Werner Bischof: Magnum

LITERATURE

The writer today is the great Japanese hero. He is followed in the streets by autograph-hunters, his face is on the magazine covers, his every activity is reported by the press. His rewards are correspondingly heroic: in 1956, for example, four novelists enjoyed higher incomes than any movie actor, entertainer or professional athlete, and since the war novelists have frequently led the entire country in income. From the newspapers (which publish at least two serialized novels daily), from the hundreds of literary magazines, and from the huge film industry pours an increasing stream of commissions which gives work not only to the famous writers but to innumerable second-raters and even hacks.

The output of the novelists, geared to this demand, is often prodigious; one famous writer has already published ninety-six novels and is said to be able to write the equivalent of ten thousand words a day with ease. The public's enthusiasm for novels seems to grow all the time. A hundred thousand copies is not an unusual sale for a popular work. At least three or four books each year sell over three hundred thousand copies. It is small wonder that when a Japanese youth announces to his parents his intention of becoming a novelist he is likely to meet with encouragement.

The elevation of the novelist to his present eminence seems to be largely a post-war phenomenon. A product of the development of mass media, it has in turn contributed to this development. For example, during the seven years that one historical romance was being serialized in a weekly magazine, the circulation shot up from about a hundred thousand to several million. Of course, publication of the novel was not the only cause of this sensational increase, but the successive episodes were read with much the fervor aroused in the United States by the comic strip.

The amazing success of serialized fiction has been explained by some sociologists in terms of the long hours spent in streetcars and trains by Japanese commuters. This theory does not explain, however, why the Japanese turn to literature as a time-killer rather than, like millions of commuters elsewhere, to newspapers or crossword puzzles. Probably it is an expression of the age-old respect for literature and for the "better sort" of writing, a preference which is otherwise demonstrated by the fact that the most authoritative newspaper rather than the sensational tabloids enjoys by far the largest circulation.

Authors elsewhere are apt to envy the extraordinary popularity of literature in Japan today and the large number of Japanese who can make a living solely by writing. The insatiable public appetite for books, however, supports many writers only to destroy them, for the necessity of feeding daily installments into the maws of the press usually prevents authors from revising or even maturely considering their work. It is almost unthinkable for a famous novelist

140 *The garden of the Ryoanji Temple in Kyoto consists of fifteen stones rising like islands out of carefully raked waves of sand. The stark simplicity of such gardens was inspired by Zen ideals.*

to let a year go by without a new book, and even senior, prosperous writers frequently produce two or three books a year. Not only do the novelists publish large quantities of fiction, but the older ones grind out volumes of reminiscences (or even publish pages from old diaries), and the younger ones essays on political and economic problems. Writers are also much in demand for lecture tours and radio appearances, both of which pay surprisingly well. Some of the more popular figures are reputed to have factories which employ talented young writers whose works are published under the great man's name. When one famous novelist of the 1930's died, so many stories commissioned by him were still being written that his "posthumous works" continued to be published for years.

Though modern Japanese literature ranks among the important branches of contemporary writing, it goes back only to the introduction of Western influence after the Meiji Restoration. Japanese literature of the period immediately preceding this revolution was undistinguished if not debased; after almost 250 years of self-imposed isolation the Japanese had drained themselves of new ideas, and foreign literary influences were accordingly welcomed with eagerness. The Japanese were obliged to pass through an era of translation, followed by one of imitation; only then were they ready to produce a new literature enriched but not dominated by foreign influences. In the domain of poetry, for example, translations of Tennyson's "Charge of the Light Brigade" and Gray's "Elegy" fascinated Japanese of the 1880's, and before long these were followed by Japanese versions of modern French and English poetry. The influence of such works showed itself in the composition by Japanese of poems much longer than the traditional *tanka* (thirty-one syllables) or *haiku* (seventeen syllables).

More important than the mere matter of length, however, Japanese poets were freed of the necessity of restricting their poetic utterances to the kind of sentiments which can be expressed in short verses. Parts of their experience which required more ample scope could now be tapped, and by the early twentieth century poets were writing in this vein:

> *I believe in the heretical teachings of a degenerate age,*
> *the witchcraft of the Christian God,*
> *The captains of the black ships, the marvelous land*
> *of the Red Hairs,*
> *The scarlet glass, the sharp-scented carnation,*
> *The calico, arrack and* vinho tinto *of the Southern*
> *Barbarians...*

This poem generates an atmosphere which could not be evoked by a mere seventeen syllables, but even the poets who still preferred the old forms felt

141 *Gracefully curved, red-painted bridges are almost a symbol of Japan. The Japanese love gardens, and many are like this one—with a cherished waterfall, a pond, and a bridge.*

ELIOT ELISOFON

free now to use modern words, and to describe their most poignant emotions:

> *Going into a vacant house once,*
> *I smoked a cigarette,*
> *Only because I longed to be alone.*

42   *Cherry blossoms scatter*
among the tall lanterns of Ueno
Park in Tokyo.

In the novel, the emphasis on the importance of the individual which had long been a mark of European fiction could be transferred to Japan only with difficulty because no such tradition existed. Rousseau began his *Confessions* with the assertion that though he might not be better than other men he was at least different; the Japanese writer would more likely have felt that though he did not differ from other men he was at least better. Yet the Japanese, affected by so many other Western ideas, could not remain indifferent to the idea of the uniqueness of the individual. The so-called "I novel," extremely popular in recent years, has been one Japanese attempt to create a novel which reveals the individuality of the author. "I novels" are often such minutely accurately descriptions of the author's own experiences that one must be interested in the author even before one begins to read his book if it is to give pleasure. Some "I novels" possess hardly any form, lacking even the selection of material which is the mark of a good autobiography; nevertheless, they are recognized in Japan not only as a possible means of expression but as a particularly serious and important one. Some authors who publish popular novels in the newspapers redeem themselves in the eyes of the literary profession by an occasional "I novel." Like the camera, the "I novel" gives an illusion of individuality by recording moments which might otherwise have dissolved unnoticed, but the problem of creating a more convincing kind of individuality still remains to be solved.

In recent years Japanese literature has aroused wide interest abroad. Many Western readers find in the translations of the modern Japanese novels a sensitivity to nature and to the play of the emotions which has been characteristic of Japanese literature since ancient times. Even in works which contain nothing of cherry blossoms or tear-soaked sleeves, a Japanese sensibility seems to be working in the techniques and presentation of otherwise modern material. The Japanese have now emerged from their period of apprenticeship to Western literature, and may before long be influencing writing elsewhere in the world.

THEATER AND DANCE

Japanese theater and dance—the two have always been intimately connected in Japan—are very old. We know that masked, comic dances were introduced from China in the eighth century and were a regular feature of temple festivals.

Some of them seem to have been indecent, and the Japanese court, fearful lest its newly-won dignity be impaired by frivolous spectacles, bestowed its patronage on a subsequently imported variety of dances called *bugaku*.

Though these dances were introduced from China and Korea, they may be of Central-Asian and Indian origins. The *bugaku* repertory consists chiefly of solemn dances offered as prayers for the prosperity of an emperor, or to celebrate the triumph of a warrior-king. The dancers wear elaborate, strikingly un-Japanese robes, and their faces are covered with grotesque masks. *Bugaku* and its strange orchestral music of flutes, pipes, drums and strings, transports the spectator to a distant world not easily reached through literature or the other arts; it is as if he suddenly found himself at the court of some Central-Asian monarch in a time known only as "long ago."

After 1200 years these dances are still performed today approximately in their original form. At the Kasuga Shrine in Nara one may watch *bugaku* danced at night on the raked sand of an inner courtyard, with the vermilion fence of the shrine and towering cedars for a background. The spectators sit in the darkness of shrine buildings illuminated only by the occasional glow of a Japanese standing lantern. The musicians begin to play the far-away harmonies, and the dancers slowly, deliberately, step out onto the moonlit sand. The hieratic gestures, the rustle of brocade robes, and the glints thrown off by their heavy masks belong to a world and a tempo completely unlike our own.

Even people of former times, however, could not have considered *bugaku* a lively entertainment. We have some accounts of the kind of performances the common people attended. There were acrobatic acts; one consisted of two men who balanced poles on their chins between which was suspended a rope crossed by a dancing girl on high heels who juggled balls. There was sword-swallowing, men who lay on beds of nails, dwarfs, magicians, and performing monkeys. There were comic playlets too: the first visit of a rustic to the capital, a nun who begs for swaddling clothes, and some decidedly improper skits.

Performances were given at shrines together with sacred dancing. Other religious observances included the simple imitation of the movements of seed-planting, accompanying prayers for a bountiful harvest. Gradually these ceremonies developed into stylized dances performed by professional entertainers, who were attached to the different shrines. As early as the twelfth century such men began making improvements on the simple festive plays, and eventually created the form of the Nô drama. In the fourteenth century the genius of two men, Kannami (1333–1384) and his son Zeami (1363–1443), lifted these rather elementary entertainments to the level of great art by charging the dialogue with magnificent imagery derived from the classical literature, and lending symbolic importance to what otherwise might be only fragmentary representations.

Many Nô plays begin with a priest on a journey to some holy spot. There

143–144 *Katsura Palace i Kyoto, a jewel of Japane architecture, was built in tf seventeenth century for tf younger brother of the Emperf Goyoze*

143 MARIANNE STEINER

144 MARIANNE STEINER

he meets a person whose strangely poetic words belie a humble appearance. The priest questions the unknown reaper or old woman, who gradually reveals the story of his former glory, and leads us to understand that some unsatisfied attachment to the world has kept his spirit behind. In the second part of the play, the same character returns in his true appearance as a great warrior or a beautiful woman, and in a final dance, towards which the whole action of the play has been pointing, re-enacts the climactic moment of his life. At the end of the play a hope of deliverance from the attachment is offered, and the ghost fades away. This form, developed chiefly by Zeami, enabled a playwright to give a poetic and complex story in a very abbreviated compass.

In some respects the Nô suggests ancient Greek drama: the fewness of the characters, the chorus, dances and masks, and an abundant use of traditional or legendary themes. However, Zeami made of the Nô essentially a symbolic theater, where both the texts of the plays and the gestures of the actors were intended to suggest unspoken, indefinable realities, the relation of the expressed part to the whole being like the visible surface to the entire iceberg. Zeami was not only the greatest author at the Nô theater, but its finest actor and most perceptive critic.

Nô soon came under the patronage of the shogunate. In 1374 the youthful shogun, Yoshimitsu, witnessed a performance in Kyoto by Kannami and the boy Zeami, who was then eleven, and was so entranced that he became an enthusiastic admirer of Nô. Court patronage enabled Zeami to write in the elevated manner he preferred, for he could be sure that his audience would catch his allusions and respond to his symbolism. The spectators were connoisseurs able to detect the slightest variation—good or bad—from the usual stage movements or sounds.

In time the traditions became so strongly entrenched that Nô developed almost into a ritual, and the audiences were so well versed in the texts that it was unnecessary and even undesirable to make the plays dramatically convincing. The dialogue was pronounced in a deliberately muffled manner, and the gestures became completely stylized. A hand slowly lifted to the face denoted weeping, the stamp of a foot might mean that a ghost had disappeared. All parts were taken by men who, even when appearing as women, used their natural deep voices and made no obviously feminine gestures.

Nô plays were intended primarily for aristocrats, but by the end of the sixteenth century other types of theater, designed for commoners, had come into being. These included the Kabuki, today Japan's most popular dramatic art.

The origins of the Kabuki are traditionally traced back to a woman dancer named Okuni who first performed her rather indecent dances—the word *kabuki* seems originally to have meant anything eccentric, and later acquired sexual overtones—in Kyoto in 1596. She won such success that soon she was performing with her troupe in other parts of the country. The suggestive

145 *Matsubayashi Keigetsu, one of Japan's greatest painters of the traditional "southern style" (nanga), paints poetic landscapes typical of his school.*

aspects of Kabuki performances apparently worried the government, and in 1629 it forbade the presence of women on the stage. Kabuki accordingly became an all-male theater, but before long the handsome young actors were attracting improper advances from the spectators, and in 1652 the Young Men's Kabuki was also banned.

Until this time Kabuki consisted almost entirely of dances whose success was dependent on the good looks of the performers, but when beauty was banished from the stage, it became necessary to interest the audiences with dramatic stories. Dancing has remained, however, an indispensable element of the Kabuki, though usually less as a set piece than as a stylized series of movements which accompanies dramatic actions.

The Kabuki is pre-eminently a theater of actors, and when Kabuki is discussed it is generally in terms of actors—the ninth Danjuro, the seventh Koshiro, the sixth Kikugoro, and so on. Some of the most famous Kabuki plays have nonsensical plots which (like those of European operas) are tolerated because of the opportunities they afford for the display of an actor's virtuosity. The high points of a Kabuki play—the places where the audience applauds or cries out its approval—are not those which depend on the excellence of the text (such as an impassioned speech), but are usually moments of no action at all, when, for example, the actor expresses his wrath, resolution or some other powerful emotion by assuming a grotesque stance.

Unlike the Nô, masks are not used in Kabuki, but many parts require heavy make-up, with a dead-white paint for women or young men, and brilliantly colored lines for the heroes of "rough business." All parts, as in the Nô, are taken by men. Kabuki actors who take the parts of women speak in falsetto and their gestures are considered to embody the essence of femininity even more than those of real women. The formal gestures of the female impersonators are so much a part of Kabuki that it is almost impossible to imagine their parts played by women.

In general, the resources of Kabuki have been directed away from representational drama: the use of men for women's parts, the highly stylized dance-movements, and the exaggerated delivery of the lines all contribute to the conspicuously theatrical, unrealistic nature of the performance. Earle Ernst observes in his excellent study, *The Kabuki Theater,* "The Kabuki audience is at all times completely, consciously aware that it is in a theater seeing a play." Because it does not expect literal truth it willingly accepts a seventy-year-old man in the part of a bashful young maiden, and many spectators will even say in retrospect that he looked more beautiful than a real girl, though a photograph would not confirm this. Through non-representational means, a kind of theatrical magic, even a hoarse-voiced old man may seem quite seductive.

Other noticeably non-representational moments occur in some scenes of the Kabuki plays, as when the performers move their bodies jerkily, describing

146 The fine art of printing from woodblocks is still practiced in Japan. Craftsmen reproduce masterpieces of the Ukiyoe artists of the seventeenth and eighteenth centuries, as well as contemporary work.

the bare outlines of their actions. This is a heritage from the puppet theater, a dramatic art almost exactly as old as Kabuki.

At one time the puppets were far more popular than actors, and the greatest Japanese playwright, Chikamatsu Monzaemon, wrote for them. The puppet theater has three elements: the puppets themselves, a chanter who narrates their dialogue and describes their actions, and a samisen player who accompanies the narrations. A first-rate performance demands not only excellence in each of the three branches of the art but flawless cooperation. This seldom-realized ideal can provide a unique theatrical experience. Because the puppet, unlike the actor, has no personality of its own, when it performs we see not an actor impersonating some famous personage, but the personage himself.

It may be almost impossible to believe that the curiously proportioned puppets can create an impression of life, particularly when their manipulators work in full view of the audience. Yet the illusion is regularly achieved, and when a puppet impatiently stamps off the stage at the end of a scene, the audience is made to feel that the puppet is dragging its three operators.

To an even higher degree than the Kabuki, the puppet theater is non-representational. There is none of the effort that puppet and marionette operators in the West bestow on convincing us that we are watching real people perform. On the contrary, Kabuki actors imitate the unrealistic but intensely dramatic gestures of the puppets. It is illuminating to see the same scene of a play performed by Kabuki actors and puppets. In *The Love Suicides at Sonezaki,* for example, the hero hides under a porch while his sweetheart sits with one foot dangling over the edge; he takes her foot and passes it across his throat to signify his intent of committing suicide. In the Kabuki version there is something indescribably erotic about the moment; in the puppet theater, on the other hand, the same gesture has the cold horror of the guillotine. The puppet theater is thus the ideal medium for a dramatic work with literary merit, for it scrupulously follows the text; the Kabuki depends on the personalities of the actors to hold an audience, and sometimes a well-written play, which forces an actor to talk instead of to act, may seem excessively wordy. It is significant that nowadays, when the younger generation finds it increasingly difficult to follow the old-fashioned language of the puppet narrator, the audiences for puppet plays are small, while the Kabuki Theater in Tokyo is full at virtually every performance.

The Kabuki is one of the most satisfying spectacles in the world. The eye is delighted not only by the performers, but by the costumes, the elaborate scenery, and the dazzling expanse of stage. There is dancing and pantomime to enchant even the foreigner ignorant of the language, and the many different varieties of accompaniment offer a panorama of the musical styles of the past three hundred years. It is small wonder that in the 1880's the first Japanese to see Western-style plays were bored and irritated by the dull spectacle of people sitting around drably-furnished rooms talking interminably.

47 Aizu Yaichi, a master of calligraphy, a major art in Japan, examines versions of several Chinese characters.

Even in recent years the modern theater has only rarely drawn large audiences. A month is a long run for a play in Tokyo even at a tiny theater, and most cities of the provinces can support only one-night stands. The actors are organized into troupes which stage a number of plays each year, some new, others revivals, and still others translations of foreign works. The plays of Chekhov probably show the modern Japanese theater at its best. The gloomy atmosphere is apparently congenial to the young intelligentsia who are the steadiest patrons of this theater—perhaps because they see resemblances between themselves and the characters on stage. Performances of *Hamlet, Macbeth* and other plays of Shakespeare in new colloquial translations have been artistically successful and show a surprising power to excite audiences.

A Japanese living in Tokyo or one of the other large cities has a choice of theatrical entertainment unrivaled in the world. At different times of the year he may see ancient court dances, the Nô, Kabuki, puppet plays, modern theater, Western and Japanese opera, as well as a variety of strip-tease shows and other light amusements. In the country, however, the films are by far the most important source of entertainment. In any small town on a quiet evening, one may be startled to hear Western voices snarling through the back wall of a cinema, and the firing of rifles as Indians bite the dust. A century ago Japanese living outside the cities could hardly have hoped to witness any entertainments but those of the annual festivals, but today the same films which enchant and bore audiences from Tulsa to Timbuktu reach the remotest regions of Japan.

However, by no means all of the films shown are foreign importations. In 1956 Japan passed the United States as the world's leading producer of motion pictures, and when one considers the relatively limited sale of Japanese films abroad, one can imagine how devotedly they are received at home. Cinemas are generally so packed that some members of the audience are obliged to stand through both features of a double bill.

Most Japanese films are at least as bad as those produced abroad. A great many deal with heroes of a century or more ago; the climax of such films is likely to be a scene in which the hero, confronted by fifty or a hundred armed men, slashes them down one after another with his trusty sword, then strides off to claim the distressed maiden who has occasioned his deeds of prowess. Films on modern subjects are likely to be better, but too often they reveal the extraordinary haste with which Japanese films are made and distributed. Nevertheless outstanding films are produced each year, and a number of them have won international prizes. The best examples show how traditional Japanese artistry can be applied to this modern medium, whether in the aesthetic composition of a scene or in the occasional use of older stage techniques.

The Japanese have yet to make any notable contributions to radio and tele-

148 *Writers are popular heroes in Japan; everyone is interested in the life of a leading novelist like Tanizaki Junichirô, shown here at home with his wife*

149 *(Over) The earliest Japanese theater probably looked much like this contemporary performance, staged outdoors in a country district*

150 *(Over) During the cherry blossom festival in Kyoto, geisha dance and act in Kabuki plays although Kabuki is traditionally performed by men*

151 *(Over) A Nô actor, masked and in ceremonial robes, lifts his lance in the role of a great warrior*

214

HIROSHI HAMAYA

149

150

152

Dennis Stock: Magnum

153

154

155

Iwanami Shoten

vision. A foreigner watching Japanese television may feel uneasily that he is seeing an old American program though Japanese programs are fortunately not as stringently controlled by commercial considerations. Television sets are now found in many middle-class households, and as their use spreads, we may hope for some of the same successes with this medium that the Japanese have already achieved in the films.

POLITE ACCOMPLISHMENTS

In contrast to the entertainments aimed at large audiences, other arts in Japan make their appeal to the discriminating few. Some, like certain varieties of Japanese dance and music, have long been considered a part of the prenuptial training of young ladies. Girls of good family were once expected to play the *koto*, an instrument rather like a zither, and some even became dancers—so skilled that they were awarded "an artistic name" by the head of the school they studied in. In recent years these accomplishments have gone somewhat out of fashion. Today well-bred young ladies are expected to play the piano, and many more of them study ballet than the traditional dances. Though they may be unable to tie the sash of their own kimonos, many can struggle through a Haydn piano sonata, execute a set number from *Swan Lake,* and talk with feeling about Renoir and Dufy. The outsider may regret the sacrifice of traditional excellence in favor of watered-down derivations of Western culture, but the importance of musical proficiency, whether on the *koto* or the piano, is usually dictated by the same unmusical considerations of enhancing a girl's marriage possibilities.

Two traditional accomplishments are still very much in vogue—flower arrangements and the tea ceremony. In flower arrangement, as in every other Japanese art, one's school is important, and a girl who studies the techniques of an unfashionable school labels herself as behind the times, if not downright dowdy. The differences are apparent even to a novice: the older schools still insist on the traditional arrangements on three levels, "heaven, earth and man," but some modern schools tend to make the flowers almost superfluous, arranging, for example, one lonely carnation in an immense concrete tank. Vegetables, withered branches, vines and grasses, as well as flowers, are used in the arrangements, making it possible for a woman to decorate her *tokonoma* at any season of the year without recourse to hothouse flowers.

An ability to perform the tea ceremony is another mark of a cultivated young lady. Many deep philosophic meanings have been read into this ceremony by its admirers, and it is certainly impressive and beautiful to watch when performed by a master. The perfection of his movements, absolutely devoid of unnecessary gestures, contributes to the tranquillity of the atmos-

152 *Great playwrights have written for the Japanese puppet theater* (Bunraku); *the puppets create a remarkable illusion of life, even though their operators are in plain sight.*

153–155 *The great Kabuki actor Nakamura Kichiemon in a "head-inspection scene" from the play* Moritsuna's Camp. *He lifts the head, turns it around and discovers to his amazement that it is not his brother's.*

phere, and requires not only a good deal of practice but an understanding of the aesthetic principles involved.

The tea ceremony is of Zen origin in its every particular—the beverage was imported from China by Zen monks, the cups were first made by potters guided by other monks, and the teahouse itself is the descendant of the hut in which one famous Zen priest used to sit in meditation. There is thus ample justification for those who consider the tea ceremony to be more than a polite accomplishment, a genuine art. However, as practiced today, it often seems hardly more than a parody of its original form. Instead of three or four guests quietly sipping tea together in a simple, almost insignificant building, "tea meetings" today generally involve large numbers of people, dressed in holiday finery, eagerly pushing into tea huts erected by masters at almost prohibitive cost.

The tea utensils were originally the least conspicuous kind of bowls, kettles and whisks, but though simplicity is still admired today, the implements may be very expensive. Many people will buy an irregularly-shaped bowl of crude pottery, not because it is less pretentious than a fine porcelain bowl, but because it boasts a long history, or has been made by a famous modern potter whose name is proudly inscribed on the box. Thus a bowl of coarse clay may cost a thousand times more than one of porcelain.

The young lady who studies the tea ceremony learns to perform each of the prescribed gestures in the manner dictated by her particular school. Whether she places the brocade napkin to her left or right will reveal the school, and here again it is important that she chooses a fashionable one. The cynic may find the tea ceremony performed today by most Japanese young ladies about as spiritually challenging as afternoon tea poured by a London matron; yet even if the Japanese girl has learned every movement by rote, with no comprehension of the satisfying order of the whole ceremony, the observer cannot but be struck by momentary glimmerings of a beauty which has the marks of long tradition. The very fact that a modern girl has learned to perform the prescribed motions of a ritual and senses, however imperfectly, their importance, is an intimation of how Japanese traditions survive today and are likely to survive in the future. Despite its commercial aspects, the tea ceremony responds to something deeply felt by the Japanese—perhaps a desire, originating in Shinto worship, to share sacred offerings with other believers, perhaps a preference for the simple, understated expression found in every Japanese art which has been touched by Zen Buddhism, or perhaps the love of order and decorum inspired by Confucianism.

Its survival today, when some traditional arts are losing their popularity and others are becoming tinged by Western influences, should afford comfort to those who bewail the passing of the old ways, and pleasure to those who prize the unique variety of old and new to be found in living Japan.

156 Hamlet (Akutagawa Hiroshi) berates Gertrude (Sugimura Haruko), in a recently translated version of Shakespeare's masterpiece.

157 A melodrama about a young samurai is performed for television.

158 (Over) The utensils of the tea ceremony.

156   TAKENORI TANUMA

SHIGEICHI NAGANO: CHUOKORON-SHA

158   Japanese Consulate General, New York

INDEX